DISCOVERING THE BIBLE:

A 13-WEEK LIFE-CHANGING JOURNEY

CLAYTON CLOER

Baptist University Press
5400 College Dr.
Graceville, FL 32440
www.bup.buf.edu

Paperback ISBN: 979-8-9937291-1-4
Hardcover ISBN: 979-8-9937291-2-1

TABLE OF CONTENTS

Chapter 1
LEARNING TO STUDY THE BIBLE

I started reading in Genesis, the first book of the Bible. In less than an hour, I was introduced to Adam, Eve, the serpent, sin, death, the tree of life, angels, clothing, Cain, Abel, Seth, Enosh, Enoch, Noah, Shem, Ham, Japheth, a global flood, the rainbow, the confused languages over the planet, and the Lord of heaven and earth. For the next few hours, the story focused on Abraham and his family. The life experiences with God of Abraham, Isaac, Jacob, and Joseph developed the storyline of the rest of Genesis. Book by book new characters, descendants of these men, were introduced and described as God interacted with them. I got lost in all the names and places and events and twists and turns in the narrative.

I soon gave up and turned to the part of the Bible with Jesus in it, the Gospels. While the setting, background, and culture was distant to me, I experienced a dynamic familiarity with Jesus' teaching, authority, and life. God spoke to me through these words. I believed in Jesus. I trusted that he died for my sin and was raised from the dead to give me eternal life. My heart was changed, my sin forgiven, and my life mission settled. The Bible came alive every time I read it. However, I struggled to understand it and be certain that I could read and study it for myself.

My father gave me a Thompson Chain reference Bible that had topics identified from most verses that linked to other verses across Scripture that addressed that topic. I studied my Bible with a topical approach, studying topics from the Bible by examining different verses that relate to the topic. For example, the topic of Abraham, introduced in Genesis 12, launched me into reading passages in the Gospels, Romans, and Galatians about Abraham. I enjoyed studying prayer through all the passages that mentioned prayer. Topical study helped me learn biblical truth, but I still did not know the Bible.

The best approach to studying the Bible is expositional. The expositional study of Scripture involves studying the Bible book by book, verse by verse, and line upon line. Some call this inductive Bible study. God delivered His Word to us book by book, verse by verse, line upon line, and word for word. Therefore, we should study the Bible the way in which it was delivered. A student needs to understand the verses of a book in the context of the book and the book in the context of the Bible. Then, a student can gain an understanding of the Bible and its contents.

God called me to ministry. I enrolled in seminary, studied the Bible day and night, and was instructed on how to study using the expositional method. Soon, others asked me to teach the Bible. I started very small with a few students and wrote the first edition of what you are reading. I have updated it throughout the years, and I owe a special thank-you to First Baptist Church of Bonifay, FL for allowing me to test this completed study on them!

THE FUNNEL PROCESS

I begin by teaching you a simple funnel process to study any passage in the Bible. You will be equipped to take the passage through a series of questions that function like unwrapping a present to reveal the meaning of the passage for the reader today.

I discovered that you can't understand the Bible unless you understand the background of the Bible. The **first layer** to be unwrapped is the **background**. The background covered thousands of years, different cultures and continents, different systems of government, family styles, worship venues and prescribed elements of worship. The geographical background needs to be understood by the reader to grasp meaning. The agrarian background in a civilization built around the land and its crops is so distant from most of us. Our study will expose you to a depth of background issues that unlock meaning in the text.

The **second layer** of this process is to uncover the **context** of the passage. The Bible was given to us in 66 books. Each book has a context and a volume of material revealed throughout its corpus. Any given story has a context before and after that must be revealed before a true understanding can be gained. Just as the words of Franklin Roosevelt: "December 7, 1941, a day that will live in infamy" cannot be understood without understanding what happened on that day, so the words of Jesus: "My God My God why have you forsaken me" cannot be understood without context. The trees can distract from the forest - the actual passage studied needs to be seen in a broader context. This study will uncover these realities and equip the reader to understand and simplify them.

The **third layer** in this funnel approach is to understand the **syntax** of the passage. Syntax means the way the words are put together. I could speak a sentence to you using the same words but have a completely different meaning. "Give us this day our daily bread" from the Lord's Prayer in Matthew 6:11 could mean that you are asking for today which is our daily bread, for daily bread for this day, or for the Lord to graciously supply our needs greater than just a ration of bread for today. Each word has a meaning, but each word also has a role in the thought. In English, a word may be a noun, a verb, an adverb, an adjective, a pronoun, and others. The verbs can then appear in different ways such as infinitives, participles, subjunctives and as different times such as future, present, or past. These sentences can also appear in a paragraph of encapsulated meaning like a parable or allegory. Therefore, the reader must learn how to spot these differences and determine their significance.

The **fourth layer** in this funnel approach involves examining **each word** and especially the verbs. The Lord inspired the words themselves. The action in the passage is revealed in verbs. The biblical authors used words from three languages which are translated into English. When you understand the process to uncover the richness of the original language then the Bible will come alive with meaning. A reader is tasked with defining words from these ancient documents. Words that we pass over as common become exceptional and profound. For example, in John 3:3, Jesus told Nicodemus that "unless you are born again then you will not see the kingdom of God." The word translated "again" has a near cognate also translated "again." The English language does not give the reader another option for the word whereas the Greek language offers two words: "again" of the same kind and "again" of a different kind. The word that Jesus used was "again" of a different kind.

This book will describe the process and develop the reader into an able interpreter by clarifying and simplifying each of these layers. The **fifth layer is the genre** or the type of writing in which the passage is found. The Bible is a literary masterpiece with distinct types of writing that have their own rules for interpreting. Parables must be treated differently than proverbs, prophesies distinct from epistles, allegories different than apocalyptic material. Each writing style conveys meaning and life-changing revelation while involving skill to understand. The Apostle Peter wrote and highlighted the needed skill in interpreting concerning the writings of Paul: "some things in them that are hard to understand, which the ignorant and unstable twist to their own destruction" (2 Peter 3:16 ESV). Ecclesiastes, Job, Hebrews, Acts, and the Psalms can only be understood in light of the genre. Each book is different, and passages may be different in chapters of a book.

The **sixth layer** of the funnel balloons the passage into the **theology or the rest of the Bible**. While a passage has one context inside of the book, for example Genesis 4 is in the context of the book of Genesis, the passage also has a context inside of all 66 books of the Bible. What does the rest of the Bible say about Cain and Abel. Jude, Hebrews, 1 John, Matthew and Luke give further insight into the events of Genesis 4. The theological implications and interpretations become clearer for a given passage like Genesis 4 when the rest of the Bible speaks to clarify and codify the meaning. Just as the modern location of Pearl Harbor has meaning as a historical event in the minds of an American and a current military and tourist location, Bethlehem had a meaning to the first century audience beyond just a location. When we say Gettysburg or Ground Zero, then we evoke not only the name of a physical location but a set of events. When we say that a politician is spending a lot of time in Iowa then we know they are considering a presidential bid. Otherwise, Iowa has little political significance. Scripture has people, events, places, and significance beyond just the words because of what the rest of the Bible uncovers for the reader. The reader must also look at theological constructs in light of the rest of the Bible.

Jesus viewed the Scriptures as a whole when He said, "And beginning at Moses and all the Prophets, He expounded to them in all the Scriptures the things concerning Himself (Luke 24:27)" and also, "You search the Scriptures, for in them you think you have eternal life; and these are they which testify of Me (John 5:39)." What is taught about this single subject elsewhere in Scripture? I will expose many of these in a fun chapter concerning the rest of the Bible.

Finally, the **seventh layer** in the funnel process is **application**. The first six layers focus on the meaning of the original author, that is, "what" was expressed and meant when originally written. The seventh layer equips the reader to make application and determine the "so what" for today. Application involves understanding three cultures: the culture of the writer and audience of antiquity, the culture of the interpreter, and then the culture of the people to whom it is being applied. Simple meaning is a guiding principle in this layer. What can we know for certain that this passage means for us today? Upon completion of the funnel, the proper meaning and understanding is gained so that the voice of God can be heard today in the ears of the reader.

The method of instruction will be through Bible study and lessons on these layers that are put into practice while studying specified texts of Scripture. A chapter per day for the next 13 weeks will be assigned to the reader. This study assigns nine questions for a reader to answer for each of these chapters. Each lesson will refer to the passages studied and the nine questions asked. If the reader will compcte the assignments, read and listen to the lessons, and follow the guidance of the instruction then the reader will learn to study the Bible. The assigned passages and the nine questions are listed below beginning under the heading of week one.

Join me in a journey of discovery as we explore the Bible and how to study it as God intended. This book is for the new person to the Bible, for the scholar, for the student, for the pro or the joe. My 30 plus years of experience in teaching the Bible to all types of learners can help you in whatever state that you are. From a PhD to pastoring different size churches, to extensive mission work, to professor and president, these informed lessons will propel you to a life of learning, understanding, and applying the truth of God revealed in the Bible. The reader should not become discouraged if the first few weeks seem challenging. There is a lot to learn about the Bible. However, breakthrough happens normally by the fourth or fifth week and the Bible begins to open like a flower in bloom. Enjoy the challenge and the rigor of the work. God's voice and God's word is worth the journey of discovery to learn to study the Bible. Join with me as we learn to study the Bible.

SCHEDULE FOR BIBLE STUDY

Week 1

    Genesis 3

    Genesis 12

    Genesis 19

    Genesis 45

    Exodus 3

    Exodus 12

    Leviticus 16

Week 2

    Numbers 11

Deuteronomy 6

Deuteronomy 8

Joshua 2

Joshua 6

Judges 16

Ruth 3

Week 3

    1 Samuel 1

    1 Samuel 3

    1 Samuel 16

    Job 1

    Job 19

    Job 42

    2 Samuel 9

Week 4

    2 Samuel 11

    2 Samuel 12

    1 Kings 18

    2 Kings 19

    2 Kings 25

    1 Chron. 29

    2 Chron. 20

Week 5

    2 Chron. 34

    Nehemiah 2

    Psalm 1

    Psalm 51

Psalm 127+128

Eccl. 3

Proverbs 5

Week 6

Isaiah 6

Isaiah 40

Isaiah 53

Jeremiah 5

Jeremiah 33

Lamentations 3

Ezekiel 3

Week 7

Ezekiel 13

Daniel 5

Daniel 9

Hosea 7

Joel 2

Amos 7

Jonah 1+2

Week 8

Micah 5

Zephaniah 3

Haggai 1

Zechariah 14

Malachi 1

Matthew 16

Matthew 25

Week 9

    Matthew 27

    Mark 6

    Mark 14

    Luke 4

    Luke 12

    Luke 15

    Luke 21

Week 10

    Luke 24

    John 3

    John 11

    John 13

    John 17

    John 20

    Acts 4

Week 11

    Acts 20

    Romans 5

    1 Corinthians 3

    1 Corinthians 15

    2 Corinthians 5

    Galatians 1

    Galatians 4

Week 12

    Ephesians 1

    Ephesians 5

Philippians 4

1 Thessalonians 1

2 Thessalonians 2

1 Timothy 6

2 Timothy 3

Week 13

Titus 1

Philemon

Hebrews 11

James 1

1 Peter 3

1 John 1

Revelation 5

QUESTIONS FOR BIBLE STUDY

Readers are asked to read at least four assignments every week during this study. A notebook should be kept with entries for each day the Bible was studied. These entries should record the passage read, the thoughts that came from the Scripture, and the answers to these questions:

1. What are the key words, phrases, people, places, and events?

Genesis 3: enmity, Eve, your desire, eyes of both of them were opened

2. What biblical topics are addressed?

Genesis 3: original sin, salvation and the Messiah, death and suffering, evil, Satan, angels

3. What is the purpose of the book in which the passage is recorded?

Genesis: to show the origin of the world, sin, and the chosen people of God

4. Is there a command to obey?

5. Is there a promise to claim?

6. Is there a sin to avoid?

7. Is there a lesson to learn?

8. Did you learn a new lesson from this text? If so, what was it?

9. What questions do I have? What confused me?

Chapter 2
BACKGROUND

Any Text

Background

Context

Syntax

Words

Genre

Theology

Application

W e have an inside joke around the office at the University. One of our cabinet members loves carbonated water, particularly Topo Chico. On one of his trips from Graceville to Orlando for the University, he took along a twelve-pack and drank most of them on the trip down. He threw each finished longneck bottle in the backseat of his car upon finishing it. While in Orlando, we met up and he gave me a ride. I could not find a place to put my bag in the back seat because of the Topo Chico bottles. At first, I could not tell what kind of bottles they were. This experience has grown into two inside jokes. The first involves riding with him and trying to find room in the backseat for anything other than his bottles. The second makes fun of his love for carbonated water and the amount he can drink in a few hours.

Inside jokes are funny to those who understand them. Inside jokes can be difficult for those who do not know the story. Someone must explain the joke to newcomers around the office so they can join in the fun. (The cabinet member takes it in stride and enjoys the fun also!)

Readers of the Bible need to know the inside story to join in the fun. The background of the Bible must be understood for the reader to connect with the revelation. I was so confused for so long when I started studying the Bible. I did not know the geography, the timeline, the familial relationships, the movement of thought, or the different plot lines of the Bible. I could be touched by what I read, but there was also something missing for me until I understood the inside background.

Biblical authors wrote to people who knew the inside story and therefore did not explain content for a distant reader. As we study the Bible today, much of our process involves learning background and context for these messages to open the text. This chapter will focus on four important matters of background: historical, geographical, worship, and agricultural. We will close with some specific examples throughout Scripture of how these matters impact meaning. When you begin to understand these background issues then you get to join in the fun.

HISTORICAL BACKGROUND

The Bible was written over at least a four-thousand-year span of time, from creation until the end of the first century AD. The authors wrote beginning approximately in 1400 BC and concluding around 100 AD. These 1500 years brought significant changes in historical background.

Think of how America is only 250 years old and has experienced massive changes in that short period. For the first 100 years of the nation, Charleston, SC, was the fourth largest city, the wealthiest city, and the most significant national city south of Philadelphia because it was the landing place for most slaves in the nation. Today, Charleston is a small city in a small state with little significance to the nation beyond its history. Just as our places today need to be understood in context to understand their meaning, so too do places in the Bible need to be studied and understood in their historical context and time frame to understand their meaning.

Events shape history. The fall, the flood, the Tower of Babel, and the call of Abraham changed the world forever. A student of the Bible must be familiar with the history behind the events of the Bible. Think of how an historian three centuries from now would misinterpret the events of September 11, 2001 without the knowledge of the history behind the events. To understand that significant event, we must know that America partnered with Israel and was the single ally to Israel. America exported a culture of immorality. America was known as a Christian nation. Communism had crumbled in the early part of the 1990's. Islam revived around the same time as Saudi Arabia funded Islamic missionary effort in former communist nations like

Afghanistan, Yemen, Somalia, and Uzbekistan. These Islamic fundamentalists settled the areas with weak governments. Radical Islam grew in this environment. America and Israel were their greatest enemies. America was attacked by these radical elements. History allows us to interpret these events accurately.

Likewise, students of the Bible must become students of Bible history to properly understand God's revelation. This section of study intends to equip the student to be more aware of Bible history as it relates to interpreting and understanding God's Word. The following events create the skeleton for the body of the revelation. These people, places, and events create the canvas for God to reveal Himself to us.

OUTLINE OF OLD TESTAMENT HISTORY

Creation: Gen. 1

Adam and Eve and the Fall: Gen. 2-3

Noah, the ark, and the global flood: Gen. 6

Tower of Babel: Gen. 11

Call of Abraham: Gen. 12

Abraham, Isaac, and Jacob: Gen. 12-37

Joseph goes to Egypt: Gen. 37-50

Covenant people go to Egypt: Gen. 45

Moses called: Ex. 3

Plagues: Ex. 7-11

First Passover: Ex. 12-13

Exodus: Ex. 13-15

Wanderings: Ex. 15 – Deut.

Covenants: Ex. 19; Deut. 28-30

Tabernacle: Ex. 24

Joshua and Caleb: Num. 13

Joshua takes over: Joshua 1

Joshua captures the Land of Promise: Joshua 2-24

Time of Judges: Judges and Ruth

Samson, Gideon, Jephthah, Deborah and Barak

Samuel becomes prophet: 1 Samuel 1-7

Israel wants a king: 1 Samuel 8

God gives them King Saul: 1 Samuel 9

God rejects King Saul: 1 Samuel 16

David chosen by the Lord to be King: 1 Samuel 16

David becomes King: 2 Samuel 1-5

David prepares to build the Temple: 2 Samuel 7

David sins: 2 Samuel 11

David and Absalom: 2 Samuel 13-19

Solomon becomes King: 1 Kings 1

Solomon builds the Temple: 1 Kings 2-11

The Kingdom divided: 1 Kings 12; 2 Chron. 11

Northern Kingdom called Israel reigns in Samaria

All the kings were bad

Ahab and Jezebel

The ministry of Elijah and Elisha

The fall in 722 B.C. to the Assyrians

Two writing prophets - Amos and Hosea

Southern Kingdom called Judah reigns in Jerusalem

Some kings good and some bad

Hezekiah and Josiah the two most important kings

Deliverance under Hezekiah: Isaiah 36-38

The fall in 586 B.C. to Nebuchadnezzar

Isaiah, Jeremiah, Micah, Joel, Obediah, Habakkuk, and Zephaniah were all writing prophets

The fall of Judah to Babylon and going into Exile - 586 B.C.

Daniel in captivity: Daniel 1-12

Ezekiel in captivity: Ezekiel 1-39

The captivity lasts 70 years

Deliverance of the Jew's under Esther

Return to the land of Israel: Ezra 1

Temple rebuilt - 515 B.C. Ezra, Haggai preaches

Wall rebuilt - 432 B.C - Nehemiah

Malachi seeks to restore proper worship

400 years of silence

The first century AD

SCHOOLS OF PHILOSOPHY

Schools of Philosophy also drove much of the thought and worldview of the people. It will be helpful to become familiar with a few key facts about the major schools.

1) Platonism
   - 300 BC
   - Dualistic
   - Ideal/spiritual vs. real/material world
   - A body/soul contrast

2) Epicureanism
- Pleasure is the highest possible good
- God does not care about man
- No immortality of the soul
- Epicurus was the founder of this school
- This appealed to the lower classes

3) Stoicism
- Reason/Logos
- Reason is the highest good
- Opposite of Epicureanism
- Fatalistic
- Fate will have its way
- Perfect self-control was the goal
- Appealed to the upper class
- Seneca, counselor to Nero, was a stoic
- Zeno of Athens was the founder

4) Skepticism
- Not really a religion
- Truth is impossible
- No universals
- All is relative

5) Gnosticism
- Dualistic - evil created world vs good spirit world, which leads to either asceticism and legalism or total care-free living
- Salvation by special knowledge
- Knowledge is a hybrid of stoicism

- Until recently, it was believed to have been a post-Christian movement.
- In the 1940's the Nag-Hammadi, a gnostic library, was dug up in Egypt. This library had 52 separate volumes dealing with Gnosticism.
- God can only relate to humans through a hierarchy of beings.
- Matter was created by an inferior being called Demiurge, who is an unkind malevolent being.
- The only escape is through reason

Key New Testament Historical Events

1) Herod the Great
2) The birth of Jesus
3) The ministry of Jesus
4) The death of Jesus
5) The resurrection of Jesus
6) The church age dawns and expands: Acts 1-24
7) The Roman Empire and the Roman Culture in the first century AD

WORSHIP BACKGROUND

Just as it is important to understand historical background, so the student must understand the worship background of the Bible to properly understand it. Let's consider some key worship contexts in both the Old and the New Testaments.

Pre-Patriarchal Period

Adam and Eve, Cain and Abel, and Noah participated in worship experiences recorded in the Bible. They attended no Temple, knew nothing of a church building, and worshiped without the Mosaic law to inform them. Their worship included sacrifices offered to the Lord on alters constructed by these saints. Their worship was public and family centered. The Lord would judge the sacrifice and the heart of the worshiper. The Lord rewarded authenticity. Clean animals were preferred as sacrifices. Statues, or images signifying God, were not present. Great moments of life were recognized in worship experiences, although common regular worship appears to occur outside of exceptional circumstances.

Patriarchal Worship

Job, Abraham, Isaac, and Jacob worshiped the Lord. They built alters, offered sacrifices on behalf of their families, and expressed their faith through these experiences. God recognized their worship and accredited righteousness to Abraham because of faith. Prayers were offered in the context of this worship that was public.

The book of Job is not introduced as many other Old Testament books are, with information disclosing the historical context of the book. The background of the book of Job is determined by the worship practice of Job and his family. Job offered sacrifices for his entire family. This places Job in the patriarchal period before the building of the Tabernacle. An alter, a sacrifice, a regular scheduled experience, thanksgiving, and authentic adoration of the One True God without images characterized this period.

Tabernacle Worship

The Hebrews left Egypt and wandered in the wilderness led by Moses. God commanded that a Tabernacle be built for the worship and arrangement of the people. The law was given in Exodus, prescribing a tent with three rooms: an outer court, an inner court, and the holy of holies. Feasts were established and offerings were required of the people. Passover, Pentecost, and the Feast of Tabernacles (or Booths) provided the three occasions requiring the people to bring sacrifices to the priests in the outer court to be placed on the alter. The Tabernacle, by virtue of being a moveable tent, was set up in many different places until the Temple was constructed by Solomon.

Temple Worship

King David prepared to build the Temple and the Lord commissioned Solomon to construct it. God chose the place on the threshing floor of Arnon the Jebusite, just slightly north of the City of David in Jerusalem on Mount Moriah. This location had tremendous significance because Abraham's offering of Isaac and because of the plague stayed by the Lord on this spot. Solomon followed God's floor plan for the Temple, patterned around the Tabernacle with three rooms, six pieces of furniture, and carefully designed steps and gates onto the Temple Mount for the pilgrims. Solomon's Temple would remain the place of worship for the people of God until it was destroyed in 586 BC by the Babylonians.

Alters in Bethel and Dan

The Northern Kingdom of Israel chose not to worship in Jerusalem at the Temple after Solomon's death. Jeroboam did not want the ten tribes of the north to travel to Jerusalem because he feared that they would follow the King of Judah who reigned from there. Therefore, Jeroboam established two alters for worship in the Northern Kingdom territory, a golden calf in Bethel and a golden calf in Dan (1 Kings 12:28-29). He also established a feast for the people to come and sacrifice.

The Exile and the Synagogue

The Northern Kingdom was destroyed in 722 BC, and the Southern Kingdom of Judah was taken into exile in 586 BC. The Temple in Jerusalem was destroyed. The people were moved to the foreign land of Babylon and sought to maintain worship by having houses of worship called Synagogues. The Jews developed their own ways and means of worshiping without a Temple, built community life around these Synagogues, and maintained their religious identity.

Zerubbabel's Temple

When the exiles return from Babylon, Ezra and Haggai lead them to rebuild the Temple. The rebuilt model lacked the beauty and wonder of Solomon's Temple, but it did serve as the focus of true worship. This Temple was named for the High Priest who oversaw the project of rebuilding. Zerubbabel's Temple would serve the Hebrews until Herod the Great restored, expanded, and repaired it in the first century BC.

Herod's Temple

Herod the Great was the Roman Tetrarch in authority in the land of Israel from around 40 BC to 4 BC. He was called "The Great" because of his unprecedented building projects to make the land of Israel attractive to travelers and religious pilgrims. He restored the Temple, expanding the Temple Mount to the size of eight football fields, installing his own high priest, and making Jerusalem a proper setting for one of the wonders of the world, the Jewish Temple. He also built his own palaces to protect him from assassination in Masada, Caesarea by the Sea, and the Herodian. Herod the Great was extremely paranoid. The scripture records his interaction with the Magi and his murderous paranoia expressed in killing the children around Bethlehem in hopes that he would eliminate the coming Messiah (Mt 2:1-12).

Jesus would attend worship at Herod's Temple. He began and ended His earthly ministry by cleansing this "den of thieves" because of the commercialization of the worship of God. Jesus predicted the destruction of this majestic structure (Mt 24-25). In AD 70, the Roman General Titus brought the Roman army to Jerusalem to squash a Jewish rebellion and destroyed the Temple, not leaving one stone upon another. The furnishings were carried to Rome and paraded as examples of Roman domination. Temple worship ended and the Temple has never been rebuilt.

Synagogues in the First Century AD
Jewish communities built synagogues throughout the Roman empire to provide the dispersed Jews places to worship near their homes. Jews also made three pilgrimages per year to the Temple in Jerusalem until it was destroyed.

The Church

Worship in the New Testament centered around the church. The church was not a location, but a people gathered, an institution that Jesus created during His earthly ministry and empowered with the Holy Spirit after His ascension at the Pentecost after the resurrection (Acts 2). The saints of God would gather on the Lord's Day to sing, worship, pray, encourage each other, teach the word, fellowship, celebrate the ordinances of baptism and the Lord's Supper, and mobilize to fulfill the Great Commission. Unbelievers would attend these meetings and many would be converted. The churches, local visible bodies of baptized believers, sprung up in communities throughout the Roman Empire, with both Jews and Gentiles participating.

GEOGRAPHICAL BACKGROUND

God inspired the biblical writers to record places and events without thorough introductions of these places because the readers knew these places. Places had meaning that made the messages delivered and events occurring more meaningful because of the setting. If I tell you that we are going to Washington to march then you would know that I meant Washington, DC. You would know the significance of that place in American society and American government. Geography can have political significance. As we've seen, Jeroboam the son of Nebat did not want the people of the northern kingdom of Israel traveling to the Temple in Jerusalem because of the political significance of Jerusalem, the King of Judah lived there. He feared that the King of Judah would steal the hearts of the people if allowed to worship in Jerusalem.

Geography can also have security and military significance. Pearl Harbor is more than a place name, but also a strategic place name that protected the west coast of the United States. Pearl Harbor housed the Navy of the United States, dedicated to defending the west of the nation. Dan, in the Bible, is similar in that it protected the land of Israel from invasion from the north. Invaders were forced by the geography of the Holy Land to travel around the mountain of Moab and Mt. Hermon to invade the land from the north. Dan held a strategic place in the land for hundreds and thousands of years. Megiddo is another city in the north that would be one of the first locations of conflict if an invader came. The valley that the city of Megiddo overlooks is called the valley of Armageddon in the book of Revelation.

Geography can have practical significance as well. Jesus spoke of bringing your gift to the alter only to remember that you have something against your brother (Mt 5:23). Jesus commanded that the gift be left at the alter and the worshiper to go and find his brother and be reconciled before offering the sacrifice. The geographical background of this text makes it powerful. When Jesus made this statement, there was only one alter in Israel, in Jerusalem in the outer court of the Temple. The worshiper would have taken a long pilgrimage to come to that alter. In Jesus' case, he traveled approximately 70 miles of rough terrain and 3000 feet of elevation change to arrive in Jerusalem. Jesus told these hearers that the priority of reconciling with a brother before you offer your sacrifice was so great that you should make a 7-day journey back home to settle the broken relationship and a 7-day journey back to offer the sacrifice. The geography makes the enormity of this command meaningful.

I live and minister in Florida. Our geography is intertwined in our conversations. Orlando and Miami are two very different cities, with very different travel dynamics. The places of the Bible have similar differences. The reader must seek to understand these realities to understand the Bible. The Bible begins in modern day Iraq and Iran near the Euphrates and Tigris rivers, moves to the Land of Promise known as Canaan, to Egypt and back to Canaan before the Hebrews settled it (Israel after they settled it), moves to Asia Minor, and then finally to Europe.

Mountains, bodies of water, regions and nations, cities and towns, and valleys provide the setting for the events of God's revelation. We love our geography in America, and we are familiar with it. From the Rockies to the Smokies, from the Mississippi to the Rio Grande, from San Francisco to New York to New Orleans to Minneapolis, the places and topography of our great nation provide a backdrop for our life experiences. God attached His revelation to these places and events. As a reader, these biblical places must be more than just big words to have the appropriate meaning. Mountains matter to the people of God and the Bible. Mount Sinai, Mount Moriah, Mount of Olives, Mount Carmel, Mount Herman, the location of the Sermon on the Mount, the Mount of Transfiguration, Mount Nebo, Calvary, and Mount Ararat are a small group of the momentous mountains mentioned and attached to the revelation of God in Scripture.

The Sea of Galilee or Lake Gennesaret or Sea of Chinnereth, the Dead Sea or Salt Sea, the Mediterranean Sea or Great Sea, the Jordan River, The Nile River, The Red Sea, the Euphrates, the Tigris, and the crystal sea are significant bodies of water.

Cities that matter: Jerusalem, Jericho, Bethlehem, Joppa, Caesarea by the Sea, Antioch, Rome, Ephesus, Athens, Corinth, Dan, Beersheba, Megiddo, Damascus, Samaria, Shechem, Ninevah, Sodom, Megiddo, the five cities of the Philistines: Gath, Ashdod, Ekron, Gaza, Ashkelon, and then Hebron, Capernaum, Caesarea Philippi, and Philippi. These are just a small selection of the crucial cities in the Bible.

Certain islands such as Cypress, Patmos, Malta, Crete, and Silicia find their way into the narratives.

Bible lands such as Edom, Moab, Ammon, Phoenicia, Syria, Egypt, Tyre and Sidon, and Lebanon are preached to by the prophets and mentioned throughout Scripture.

Elevation changes make the land difficult to navigate. These changes impact the texts of Scripture. Jesus went through Samaria in John 4 because He intentionally sought the route. It was a much more difficult route from Galilee to Jerusalem because of elevation changes over the mountains instead of the way of the Jordan River. The vantage point and view from Mt. Carmel to the Mediterranean Sea becomes important in 1 Kings 18 when Elijah tells his servant to look for a cloud over the Sea. En Gedi is littered with caves because of the limestone rock and the rushing water coming down from the Judean hills. Saul went into one of these caves and relieved himself within arm's length of the fugitive David. Jesus descended the Mount of

Olives on a donkey colt that had never been ridden and stated that if His followers were quiet then the rocks themselves would cry out. The reader of the Bible must familiarize themselves with all these places to grasp the messages conveyed.

Agricultural Background

The land of Israel produced seven main crops which provided a background for the calendar, feasts, setting, and substance of an enormous percentage of the Bible material. Moses told the people in Deuteronomy 8:8 that they would live in "a land of wheat and barley, of vines, and fig trees and pomegranates, a land of olive trees and honey." Two grains, barley and wheat, supply the people with bread. The harvests of these grains would be the background of the feast of unleavened bread or Passover and then Pentecost. Scripture would date events by these grain harvests. Parables and comparisons would be made in the teachings of Jesus and throughout the Bible to these grains. Jesus compared his own death to a grain of wheat falling to the ground and dying. Gideon was symbolized by a barley cake. Ruth came to Boaz at the time of the barley harvest. The Temple was built on Arnon the Jebusite's threshing floor where wheat was separated from the tares.

Five fruits provided the flavor in the land: olives, grapes, pomegranates, figs, and dates. These fruits made sustaining and satisfying life in the land possible and pleasant. The land was known for production of these fruits in abundance and the ability to sustain such fertile herds, a land flowing with milk and honey. The honey referred to is not bee honey but date honey, the very best on earth.

Scripture attaches God's messages to these fruits. Jesus illustrates his relationship to His children with a grape vine and branches. Israel was an olive tree and Gentiles are wild olive branches grafted into the olive tree. Israel was likened to a fig tree that was without fruit and cursed. Isaiah wrote the parable of the vineyard. Jesus would begin His suffering in the Garden of the Olive Press (Gethsemane). The feast of Tabernacles or Booths came at the end of the fruit harvest. Gideon threshed wheat in a wine press when the Lord came to him and called him a mighty man of valor. The reader needs to understand the realities and processes of farming, growing, harvesting, and cultivating these crops to grasp the vivid images of Scripture. Resources abound to assist the reader in understanding these background areas. Commentaries, biblical encyclopedias, online resources, and study Bibles have helpful articles and insights.

Examples of Background Matters and Interpretation

"Enter His gates with thanksgiving and His courts with praise." (Psalm 100:4)

I have heard in church the words of the psalmist on many occasions: "Enter His gates with thanksgiving and His courts with praise." The background of this phrase brings the call to worship much greater and deeper meaning. The Hebrews were commanded to undertake three pilgrimages per year to Jerusalem to offer sacrifices and to worship during the feast times. Jesus, for example, would have traveled from Nazareth to Jerusalem along the Jordan River route. Jesus, Mary, Joseph, James, Jude, the other brothers and sisters and the caravan of pilgrims would have traveled through Jericho, which is 900 feet below sea level, and turned up the hill to travel 18 miles up to Jerusalem, which is 2575 feet above sea level. The journey would have taken at least five days of hard travel on foot. The shoes of the first century were a simple strip of leather between the foot and the stone paths. The journey was long, the elements of weather and terrain were difficult, and the perils of thieves and wild animals meant that a pilgrim must be determined to obey the Lord and come before Him as prescribed. Finally, at the end of at least five hard days, Jesus' family would arrive in the Holy City.

Entering the gates of the city are referred to in Psalm 100. The pilgrims were to give thanks upon that historic moment of finally arriving at the Holy City to worship after such an exhausting journey. God commanded them to be thankful that they were fit, safe, and blessed to arrive. The psalmist added that the pilgrims were to enter His courts with praise. The courts referred to in the text are the inner and outer courts of the Temple. They journeyed to the Holy City to bring an offering. They were to praise the Lord because they had something to offer, an opportunity to offer, and a God who invited them to offer a sacrifice in the context of praise to the Almighty God who sustained and blessed them.

The full weight of this simple phrase, "Enter His gates with thanksgiving and His courts with praise," can be understood only through knowledge of the background. It means more than being thankful when we get to church or as something to read to begin the service with praise. The text commands us to make a priority of collective worship, to sacrifice to be faithful to gather for worship, and to come with an expectancy and a gratitude of a pilgrim who has prepared for months to have this privilege.

"So if you are offering your gift at the altar and there remember that your brother has something against you, leave your gift there before the altar and go. First be reconciled to your brother, and then come and offer your gift." **(Matthew 5:23-24)**

Jesus was referring to the lone alter in Israel at the time, which was in Jerusalem at the Temple. The text meant much more than just walk out of church and go find your brother. The Hebrews would have gone on pilgrimages to Jerusalem from the Galilee to offer their gifts on the alter. The highest and holiest occasion would have been offering a sacrifice there. It was the culmination of a year's planning, a hard week of walking, and a significant financial investment to leave the fields and workplace to make the journey. Jesus commanded them to leave the gift at the alter in the Temple in Jerusalem and go back to the Galilee, find the brother who needs reconciliation, reconcile, then return to Jerusalem to offer the gift. Jesus placed a high priority on reconciling with a brother. The worship background of this text makes it rich with meaning and moving in application for the reader.

"And the city and all that is within it shall be devoted to the Lord for destruction." **(Joshua 6:17)** "And they came back here in the fourth generation, for the iniquity of the Amorites is not yet complete" **(Genesis 15:16)**

The Hebrews came out of Egypt and took the land by beginning in Jericho. Joshua led the people of God to conquer that great city.

The Lord spoke to Abraham in Genesis 15 and told him of the long season that His people would spend in a foreign land as slaves and then that they would emerge and take the land that Abraham had dwelt in. God said that the iniquity of the Amorites is not yet complete. God in His grace gave the Amorites many hundreds of years to repent and change their ways. They did not, and the judgment of God came down upon them in the form of complete destruction of their greatest city and the people there. The background of Genesis 15 sheds light on the reality of penial judgment revealed in Joshua 6.

Chapter 3
CONTEXT

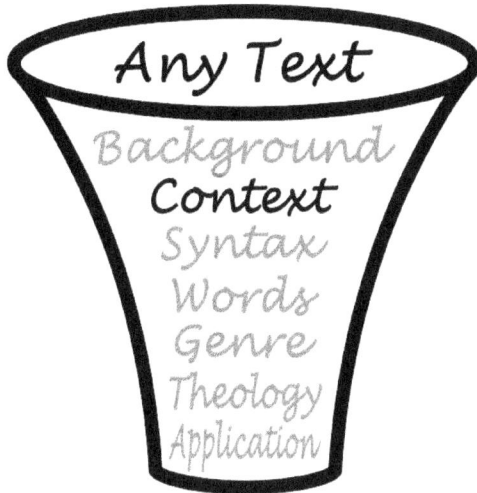

The context of a passage includes the material in the book that precedes and follows the text being studied. Context allows the reader to understand the author's original intent for the text. God delivered the Bible in written forms. While every word is inspired by God, the words occur in a context of a greater discourse or narrative. Readers need to be able to see the broader context before effectively narrowing the focus to one paragraph or verse for interpretation. The following New Testament passages illustrate the need for careful contextual analysis for proper Bible study.

CONTEXT IN THE SERMON ON THE MOUNT

The Sermon on the Mount is the longest and most famous of Jesus' sermons recorded in the New Testament. The vast material is recorded in Matthew 5-7. The key verse is Matthew 5:17-18: "Think not that I am come to destroy the law, or the prophets: I am not come to destroy, but to fulfil. For verily I say unto you, Till heaven and earth pass, one jot or one tittle shall in no wise pass from the law, till all be fulfilled." The law had to be explained to the Jews. Matthew has been systematically demonstrating that Jesus was the predicted Christ. He has presented the genealogy, explained the three prophesies of Jesus' childhood (2:15, 2:18, 2:23), introduced the ministry of John the Baptist (3:1-12), and introduced the public ministry and the location of the ministry of Jesus (4:14-16).

The Sermon on the Mount explained the law. The law was given to produce these attitudes. If one properly understood the law then he would be "poor in spirit," "mournful," "meek," "hungry and thirsty after righteousness," "merciful," "pure in heart," and a "peacemaker." Then, Jesus took the laws and presented the principles of the law. Finally, He expounded upon the principles of the law related to giving, praying, fasting, judging others, money concerns, and praying. The Beatitudes and their meaning are clearer when the context is recognized.

CONTEXT IN THE GOSPELS

Mark 6:30-52 records two miracles of Jesus: the feeding of the five thousand with two fish and five small loaves and walking on the water, also known as the loaves and the trip across the sea.

Interpreters and readers should take note that Mark explicitly explained the linkage in the two events in verse 52. These two miracles and the experience of the disciples are linked. The miracle of the loaves was a lesson to help the disciples navigate the sea in their next experience. The loaves should have changed the way in which the disciples approached their task, but they did not.

Luke 15 records the Parable of the Prodigal Son, which should be called the Parable of the Prodigal Father. The main character is the Father. The focus of the previous two parables in the chapter, the lost sheep and lost coin, is upon the joy in heaven over finding one sinner. The focus of the third parable is likewise the same, the joy of the Father for His son who was lost but is now found and who was dead and is now alive. The text also states that these three parables were actually one parable: "So he told them this parable" (Luke 15:3 ESV).

John stated the purpose of his gospel so that the reader could understand the reasons that he had for recording these events: "And many other signs truly did Jesus in the presence of his disciples, which are not written in this book: But these are written, that ye might believe that Jesus is the Christ, the Son of God; and that believing ye might have life through his name" (John 20:30-31). John 2:11 and 4:54 continue to prove that John had a clear structure for the book and that the context was critical to interpreting the book. The last six days of Jesus life are clearly traced. John 11:45-57 explained the reason He hid Himself for a time. John 12:1 explains the occasion that Jesus became known again.

CONTEXT IN THE ACTS OF THE APOSTLES

Context proves critical to understanding the book of Acts. Paul's ministry in Corinth in Acts 18 cannot be fully understood without understanding Paul's context. First, Paul came to Corinth, according to 1 Cor. 2:1-5, in fear and trembling and much weakness. Why was he so afraid? God spoke to Paul while in Corinth and told him "Do not be afraid" (18:9). The context of Acts reports to the reader that in 13:50 the Jews expelled them out of Antioch, in 14:5 they endured an assault in Iconium (an attempt to stone them), in 14:19 Paul was stoned in Lystra, in 16:22-24 they we beaten, scourged, and locked in the stocks in Philippi, in 17:10 Paul is smuggled out of Thessalonica after Jason was persecuted, in 17:14 Paul is smuggled out of Berea, in 17:16 Paul waited in Athens determined to not preach until his friends came but his spirit was stirred. Paul endured such hardship, persecution, and trials on every stop of his missionary journey that he grew afraid. He came in weakness and fear. The Lord spoke to Paul, and he stayed in Corinth for 18 months. His practice changed after his experience with the Lord in Corinth.

Peter commanded in Acts 2:38: "Repent and be baptized everyone of you for the remission of sins and you will receive the Holy Ghost." Did Peter mean that the way you are saved is through repentance and baptism? "For" (eis) can be translated "with a view to" or "because of." What does "for the remission of sins" modify? The repentance or the baptism or both? It could be either one according to the grammar. Context will have to tell the reader. When do you receive the Holy Spirit? In Acts 10:47 those that believed Peter's message clearly received the Holy Spirit before they were baptized. Peter said, "Can anyone forbid water, that these should not be baptized who have received the Holy Spirit just as we have?" People are saved by receiving God's Word rather than baptism according to the context. Acts 2:41: "Then they that gladly received his word were baptized . . .". Acts 2:44 says that those who believed constituted the early church, not those who were baptized. The conclusion is that Peter said: "Repent and let everyone of you be baptized because of the remission of sins and you shall receive the gift of the Holy Spirit."

CONTEXT IN ROMANS

Romans 9 records a controversial text relating to predestination and election. This passage is properly understood in its context. The passage has in view God rejecting his elect people (Rom. 11:1), and not the individual salvation of Jacob and Esau. God's chosen people, Israel, are not being saved because of their unbelief (Rom. 11:23).

First, the text in question addresses not individuals but the nations of Israel and Edom. The Scripture tells us that two nations were under discussion here (Gen. 25:23). The "not only this" of verse 10 points us back to the previous context in verse 9. The discussion is about Abraham's physical seed being accepted. God's election of Israel was so that he could deliver the Messiah to the world and not for individual salvation. Paul even begins to conclude this section in Romans 11:1 by asking "Has God cast away His people?" Paul was speaking of God's people, Israel, not the person of Jacob.

Second, "The purpose of God in election" has nothing to do with the individual salvation of two men but rather the family of the coming Messiah: that He would come from Isaac and Rebecca.

Third, Malachi 1:1-3, quoted in verse 13, was not written until long after both men were dead, and it referred to the nations not the men. The book of Malachi is written about these nations and is a historical statement commentating on the lives and people of these two nations, Jacob and Esau. Malachi 1:4 clarifies any confusion that this text speaks to the nations and not the men over a millennium before. Many try to claim that Jacob and Esau are types of all men, but this is unwarranted from the text and violates other teachings of Scripture. As physical nations, God blessed and preserved the Israelites even when they were rebellious so that the purpose of God in election might stand, so that His Son could be born into this Jewish people. Edom, on the other hand, was destroyed because they were not the chosen people to bring forth the Messiah.

Paul then asks: "Is God unrighteous?" The compassion spoken of in Exodus 33:19 and quoted in Romans 9:15 is manifested in the revelation of God to people. God reveals Himself specially to those whom He wishes not to the ones who earn it by works. Rather, God even revealed Himself to the Pharaoh (Romans 9:17). God preserved his life and raised him up and revealed himself to the Pharaoh and the Pharaoh hardened his heart. Then God continued to disclose himself to the Pharaoh and God hardened His heart by the revelation, just as in Isaiah 6:9-10 with Israel.

Paul asks, "Why does He still find fault?" in verse 19. Paul answers with four things: 1) who are you to ask and impugn the character of God because God does not answer to any man; 2) God has prerogatives over His creation to create one for dishonor like a potter does. This does not mean that God predestined Pharaoh's decision but rather it means that God used Pharaoh for honor for Himself because of Pharaoh's hard heart; 3) God did it to reveal more of Himself to those who would respond to it (v.23); 4) Paul concluded the question of why does God still find fault in verses 30-32: they did not pursue it by faith (v.32) because they stumbled at the stumbling stone which is Christ.

Fourth, why did the Jews not receive Christ? Paul tells us that it was because "they did not seek it by faith" (Rom. 11:32). Even clearer, Paul states: "Because of unbelief they were broken off, and you stand by faith" (Rom. 11:20). They were not lost because of God but because of their own unbelief.

Fifth, if Paul was referring to individual salvation predestined and predetermined before life, then he would have not been praying for Israel in Romans 10:1. Yet, if Paul believed that God was incapable of influencing them, he likewise would not have been praying. God draws, influences, and reveals while man must believe, receive, and respond to the offer of the free gift.

CONTEXT IN THE PAUL'S EPISTLES

First Corinthians 13, the love chapter, is embedded in the middle of the context of expressing spiritual gifts in the church. A study of the gifts must not avoid the study of love in expressing them to be true to the author's intention.

Second Corinthians 12 recorded the trip by Paul to the third heaven and the thorn in the flesh given to Paul lest he be exalted for his revelations.

Many texts are dependent on the reader performing thorough analysis of the context to open the meaning. The reader should familiarize themselves with the macro-structure of the book being studied. First Corinthians 7 and the exhortations to the virgins to remain unmarried take on a profoundly different contextual meaning if the "present distress" (7:26) is referring to war. The discussion of doing well and doing better in verse 38 has clear application in that context.

Chapter 4
SYNTAX

Any Text

Background
Context
Syntax
Words
Genre
Theology
Application

Syntax means the way the words are arranged and relate to each other in sentences, paragraphs, and books. Words possess attributes that make them serve as different parts of speech. Each sentence has an independent thought for it to be a sentence. The independent thought is then surrounded by dependent thoughts like propositional phrases, appositives, subjunctive clauses, adverbial clauses, and infinitival clauses. Verbs, nouns, adjectives, adverbs, pronouns, and possessive pronouns make up the remaining parts of the sentence. These words are arranged for emphasis, for effect, and for meaning. These words fit in a broader arrangement in a paragraph, a string of independent thoughts. Grant Osborne stated: ". . . words have meaning only as part of the larger context. Therefore, syntax is structural at the core."[1]

DEPENDENT AND INDEPENDENT THOUGHTS

The reader of the Bible must be able to recognize the main or independent thoughts in each passage and the thoughts that are subordinate or dependent to the main thought. The genre of the text, if it is narrative or epistolary, can magnify this need. Narrative text records events, reporting as the writer and Holy Spirit leads. The authors of the epistles instructed, corrected, and exhorted the believers with thoroughly structured texts to produce life change. The content in epistles generally present a more urgent need to be syntactically aware of the arrangement of the words.

For example, in Romans 12:1-2, Paul begged the believers in Rome to present their bodies as living sacrifices. "I beseech you therefore, brethren, by the mercies of God, that you present your bodies a living sacrifice, holy, acceptable to God, which is your reasonable service. And do not be conformed to this world, but be transformed by the renewing of your mind, that you may prove what is that good and acceptable and perfect will of God" (NKJV). He explained to them that such a sacrifice would be reasonable because of the things already stated concerning our salvation through the sacrifice of Christ and by the mercies of God. He added to the main thought, begging the believers to present their bodies as sacrifice, a dependent thought: "this is reasonable service." Paul asked a lot of the Christians in Rome,

[1] Grant Osborne, *The Hermeneutical Spiral: A Comprehensive Introduction to Biblical Interpretation*, Rev. Ed, (Downers Grove, IL: IVP Academic, 2010), 113.

but he clarified that the ask was because of the great sacrifice given for them and the glorious standing that they had in Christ. He then called them to refuse conformity to the world so they could embrace transformation by the renewing of their minds, which was the second dependent thought in the text. Paul added a dependent purpose clause to explain the result of the refusal to conforming to the world: "that you may prove what is that good and acceptable and perfect will of God."

In Philippians 2:12-13, in light of the monumental Christological paragraph in Philippians 2:5-11 concerning the humiliation and exaltation of the Christ, Paul gave a command to the believers: "Therefore, my beloved, as you have always obeyed, so now, not only as in my presence but much more in my absence, work out your own salvation with fear and trembling, for it is God who works in you, both to will and to work for his good pleasure" (ESV). The command, which is the main thought of these verses, is "my beloved work out your own salvation." The command is preceded by multiple dependent thoughts and then followed by other dependent thoughts. The other phrases clarify, give meaning, enhance, and support this thought. Paul is confident that they will obey because of their distinguished past of obedience. Paul used the word translated "therefore" to link to the previous paragraph on the work of Christ as an example to Christians. He explained that the motivation and the means to work out our salvation originated with God, who works in us to will and to do it

The syntax of the fourth commandment in Exodus 20 impacts the interpretation of the Sabbath observance until this day. The command is to labor for six days to remember the Sabbath and keep it holy. The command organizes the week, orders our work, and observes a day of rest and worship. The command does not specify Saturday as the Sabbath. The commandment codified that six days are given to prepare to worship, give, sacrifice, and rest on the seventh day. Sabbatarians, like Adventists today, focus on the external observance of Sabbath on Saturday. Paul wrote to the Colossians that they should let no one judge them on Sabbath day observance. The New Testament saints practiced a Sunday observance of the Sabbath. The syntax in Exodus 20:8-11 informs this discussion by clarifying that the command is to labor six days to remember. Which day of the week it is does not matter. Hank Hanegraff, author and broadcaster, stated: "The truth is, the observance of Sunday rather than Saturday does not violate God's Commandments at all! The Sabbath command in the Old Testament never specified a "Saturday" observance; rather, it was simply a command that we should observe a cycle of six days of work and then rest for one day. So obviously, the intent of the Sabbath command is kept when we rest on Saturday or on Sunday, it really doesn't matter."[2]

Steve Bright: "This view is sometimes called "Sabbatarian," but it differs from seventh-day Sabbatarianism in several respects: First, it maintains that the specification of the seventh day was part of the ceremonial aspect of the fourth commandment that was done away with in Christ, but the principle of setting apart one day in seven for

[2] Hank Hanegraaff, "Sunday Sabbath: Does Sunday Observance Violate the Sabbath?," *Perspectives*, Christian Research Institute, March 17, 2009, https://www.equip.org/perspectives/sunday-sabbath-does-sunday-observance-violate-the-sabbath.

rest and worship is part of the moral aspect and thus remains. Sunday observance, therefore, does not violate the fourth commandment and is not a sign of apostasy, as Seventh-day Adventists assert. Second, it holds that the focus of Sabbath celebration shifted from God's rest from Creation (Gen. 2:2–3), to Israel's rest from slavery in Egypt (Deut. 5:13–15), and now to the believer's final rest in Christ (Heb. 4:8–10). The Old Testament Sabbath rest was but a physical 'shadow' of the spiritual reality of the believer's rest in Christ. This Sabbath rest in Christ is now appropriately celebrated on the Lord's Day, which historically is the first day (Sunday) and not the seventh day. According to this view, 'the Old Covenant Sabbath is transformed into the New Covenant Lord's Day,' but with 'significant changes in application and practice of the fourth commandment.' The Sabbath is most appropriately kept by resting and worshiping on the Lord's Day (Sunday), though historically there has been a range of opinions about what activities are permissible."[3]

Ephesians 1:1-14 is one long sentence in the original language. The independent thought for the entire passage occurs in verse 4: "He chose us in Him." The other clauses, phrases, and thoughts orientate around this main thought. Verse three reveals that we should bless God because He has already blessed us with every spiritual blessing in Christ Jesus. The spiritual blessings imparted to us in Christ enable us for every good work and are intended to provoke us to praise God for them. We find our election in Christ. Once in Christ, we have been predestined to the adoption of sons by Jesus Christ, the resurrection

---

[3] Steve Bright, "Sabbath Keeping and the New Covenant," *Christian Research Journal* 26, no. 2 (2009; updated September 13, 2023), https://www.equip.org/articles/sabbath-keeping-and-the-new-covenant/.

from the dead. These prerogatives and privileges bestowed upon you in Christ are to the praise of the glory of His grace. In Him, we have redemption, we have the forgiveness of sins, we have obtained an inheritance, and we were sealed with the Holy Spirit of promise. All of the dependent phrases relate to the independent thought that we are chosen in Him.

The reader may choose to focus on redemption, forgiveness, predestination, sealing of the Holy Spirit, or the inheritance bestowed upon us. However, these incredible privileges and blessings, what John Stott called the golden chain, originate in Christ and in being found in Him.[4] The reader must not miss the main thought: "He chose us in Him" for looking at the subordinate thoughts: redemption, predestination, inheritance, etc.

Here are a few tips for spotting dependent thoughts:
1) A prepositional phrase begins with a preposition like in or of
2) An infinitive has a verb with the word "to" in front of it
3) A participle is a verb with an "ing" ending like "endeavoring to keep the unity of the Spirit in the bond of peace" in Ephesians 4:1
4) An adverbial phrase begins with since, while, when, or then
5) A purpose or result clause begins with "that" or "in order to" like Ephesians 2:7, "that in the ages to come He might show the exceeding riches of His grace toward in His kindness toward is in Christ Jesus."

---

[4]John R. W. Stott, *God's New Society: The Message of Ephesians* (Downers Grove, Il: InterVarsity, 1979), 32.

GRAMMAR

Syntax impacts understanding because the relationship of the words to each other clarifies meaning. Ephesians 2:8 states, "For by grace you have been saved through faith. And this is not your own doing; it is the gift of God." Some have questioned what the gift is. Is the gift salvation or is it faith? However plausible the interpretation that faith is the gift of God may seem in English, it is clear from the Greek language syntactically that Ephesians 2:8 is not referring to faith as a gift from God. For the "that" (*touto*) is neuter in form and cannot refer to "faith" (*pistis*), which is feminine. The antecedent of "it is the gift of God" is the salvation by grace through faith (v. 9). Commenting on this passage, the New Testament Greek scholar A. T. Robertson noted: "'Grace' is God's part, 'faith' ours. And that [it] (*kai touto*) is neuter, not feminine *taute*, and so refers not to *pistis* [faith] or to *charis* [grace] (feminine also), but to the act of being saved by grace conditioned on faith on our part."[5]

STRUCTURAL LITERARY DEVICES

Syntax can unite a passage and distinguish it from the immediate context. The reader can be alerted that a paragraph was intended to be understood as a whole unit. Isaiah 56:9-12 is a unit, a syntactical whole in a long prophetic discourse concerning the compromise and idolatry of the people of God. Isaiah wrote: "All you animals of the field and forest, come and eat! Israel's watchmen are blind, all of them, they know nothing; all of them are mute dogs, they cannot bark; they dream, lie down, and love to sleep. These dogs have fierce

---

[5]A. T. Robertson, *Word Pictures in the New Testament* (Nashville: Broadman, 1930), 4:525.

appetites; they never have enough. And they are shepherds who have no discernment; all of them turn to their own way, every last one for his own profit. "Come, let me get some wine, let's guzzle some beer; and tomorrow will be like today, only far better!'" The passage describes the blind and mute watchmen by comparing them to guard dogs that will not bark.

The Psalmist used structural literary devices to unite long pieces. Psalm 119 has a macro-structure dependent on an acrostic of the Hebrew alphabet. Each eight-verse segment begins with a successive letter of the alphabet. Psalm 135 used repetition of the same phrase in every verse, "for His steadfast love endures forever," to amplify the main message of the Psalm. This type of repetition in a song supplied emphasis and musical effect.

Syntax should strengthen understanding and fortify interpretation. Many passages have a distinct form of syntax that gives arrangement to the message. In Revelation 2 and 3, the seven letters to the churches follow a specific arrangement: These seven letters reveal a parallelism that is unique. Some are longer, others are shorter in size, but each letter consists of seven parts:

1) The address to each of the seven churches in Asia Minor
2) An aspect of the Lord's appearance to John at Patmos
3) An evaluation of the spiritual health of the individual church
4) Words of praise or reproof
5) Words of exhortation
6) Promises to the overcomer
7) A command to hear what the Spirit says to the churches

The unique syntax gives the reader an ability to compare these churches, contexts, and promises of the Lord. The overcomers in each case build upon one another to establish the blessing of following Christ to the finish. The overcomers will eat of the tree of life, will not be hurt by the second death, will be given the hidden manna to eat, will have power over the nations, will have their names confessed by the Lord Jesus before the Father, will be made pillars in the temple, and will sit with Jesus on His throne.

CONDITIONAL STATEMENTS

"If then" statements in the New Testament have a unique syntactical meaning compared to English. Readers may be easily confused by these when studying the New Testament. "If then" statements are prominent in the New Testament. For example, "if you love me keep my commandments" (John 14:15). The condition is the "if "clause, and the result is the "then" clause. A simple understanding of the syntax of these statements can benefit the reader. There are four classes of conditional statements.

1) First class conditional statement: the "if "clause is assumed to be true, as in Colossians 1:23: "if indeed you continue in the faith, stable and steadfast, not shifting from the hope of the gospel that you heard, which has been proclaimed in all creation under heaven, and of which I, Paul, became a minister" (ESV).

2) Second class conditional statement: the "if" clause is assumed to be contrary to the fact, or false, as in the last if then statement of John 15:20: "Remember the word that I

said to you: 'A servant is not greater than his master.' If they persecuted me, they will also persecute you. *If they kept my word, they will also keep yours*" (ESV, emphasis mine). The Jews did not keep Jesus' words. Jesus uses this second class rhetorically to enlighten the disciples of the cost of following Him.

3) Third class conditional statement: the "if" clause is assumed to be a possibility that could go either way, as in Romans 10:9: "Because if you confess with your mouth that Jesus is Lord and believe in your heart that God raised him from the dead, you will be saved" (ESV). Jesus also used 3rd class conditional statement in John 7:37: "On the last day of the feast, the great day, Jesus stood up and cried out, 'If anyone thirsts, let him come to me and drink'" (ESV).

4) Fourth class conditional statement: no biblical example exists of this class.

SYNTAX AND THE COVENANTS

Syntax shaped the revelation of the covenants in the law. The covenant principle defines the relationship of God to His people. Hebrews used the word "covenant" to describe their relationship with God from the earliest time. The word translated "covenant" comes from a word that means "to clasp or fetter." It designates a commitment or a promise that is confirmed by an oath, a pledge or agreement of binding obligation. God confirmed his relationship with His people through these binding agreements and obligations.

There are five Old Testament Covenants.

1) Covenant with Abraham – Genesis 15:1-21

2) Covenant of holiness – Exodus 19:2-4

3) Covenant of Entry – Exodus 34:10-17

4) Covenant of Possession – Deuteronomy 28-30

5) Davidic Covenant – 2 Samuel 7:12-16; Psalm 89:3-37

Exodus 19:2-4 is known as the covenant of holiness. The syntax of the passage flows in a threefold pattern.

1) Covenant stipulation – God said "if" in verse 5. This means that the condition offered to them had not already been met. It was not their ethnic nationality that brought the benefits of the covenant to them. They had to do something to gain the benefits.

2) Covenant condition – A poor English translation in verse 5 complicates the question of what the condition of the covenant is. The English has the "then" in the wrong place. The Hebrew has the "then" after "obey my voice," but the English has the "then" after "keep my covenant." The covenant condition that had to be met was to "obey My voice," which is the same thing as faith. In the Old Testament just as in the New Testament, God's people were saved by faith alone. The formula presented in the covenant condition looks like this in the text: A = B + C (A = obey my voice; B = you will keep my covenant; C = you will be a special treasure to Me above all people).

3) Covenant benefits: God said that if they trusted Him and then their works came from that faith then they would receive four benefits:

   a. We become His treasured possession (Ex. 19:5)

   b. We become a kingdom of priests (Ex. 19:6) – this speaks to our mission to the world

   c. We become a holy nation (Ex. 19:6) - this speaks to our sanctification

   d. We keep His commands – We are saved by grace through faith unto good works. They were in the covenant cause of faith, but the faith produced great works.

Chapter 5
WORDS

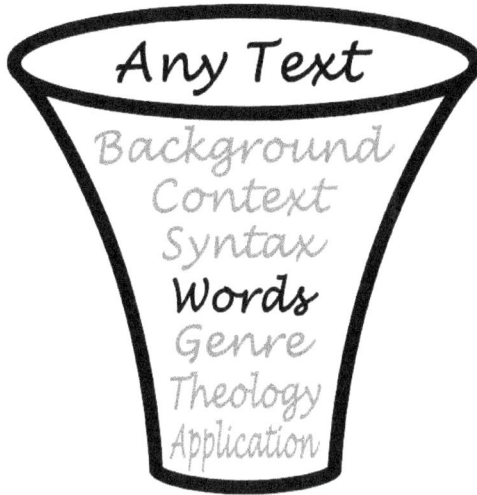

The Bible is inspired at the word level and not the paragraph or thought level. The words themselves are inspired by God. Jesus said that even the smallest strokes of a pen distinguishing each Hebrew letter were inspired by God. Paul, in Galatians, built an entire theological teaching on the singular word "seed" in Genesis 12. The words matter. Words convey meaning, carry inspiration, and move the hearer. "So then faith comes by hearing and hearing by the word of God" (Romans 10:17). Readers have to be able to determine the meaning of the words.

Words, in the Bible, perform the same function as works of art. They strike the reader with inspiration, revelation, and manifold beauty. Words bring taste and flavor, character and consistency, complexity and simplicity. Bible words became tools in the hands of God to awaken the soul of a human, light the darkest path, magnify the most hidden sin, hunt the forgotten, herald the risen King, and construct the broken spirit. God's word possesses incomprehensible power to terrorize Satan and His demons, to unlock a thickened mind, and to un-muddy the shallow waters of unfaithfulness. A reader should be struck with the privilege of reading words authored by the God who spoke: "Let there be light."

You have been asked to recognize the important words of the chapters that you have read so that you could discover the richness of these words and understand the text. Words must be carefully defined. Words can be defined in three ways: historical meaning, etymology, and usage.

HISTORICAL MEANING

The historical meaning of a word can be found in the dictionary or a lexicon if the Greek or Hebrew word is being looked up. These definitions are based on the way in which the word has been traditionally used. Two major limitations prevent the dictionary from being the best source of a definition. First, dictionaries are written by people who interpret the words. People make mistakes, and sometimes a word is improperly defined or distorted. When Saint Jerome translated the Greek word "repentance," he mistranslated it as "do penance." This one mistake created the sacrament of penance in the Roman Catholic Church, confused the meaning of repentance for untold millions of believers, and distorted the meaning of the word translated "repentance" up to this day. Some Catholic lexicons continue to translate it this way.

Second, words change meaning over time depending upon usage. Think of words like gay, cool, drip, and mouse. The word "gay" was a common term that meant happy, until the late 1970's when the word took on the meaning of same sex sexual relationships. A dictionary from the 1960's would be mistaken if consulted for the modern definition. The word "cool" is used today to mean nothing concerning temperature. It means a person is acceptable and commended, "He is cool." The word "drip" does not concern a slow-moving flow of liquid, but instead describes the attire or dress and style of a person: "I like your new drip." The word "mouse" does not mean a small rodent but a device that moves the curser on a computer screen. These words have changed in recent years.

ETYMOLOGY

Etymology examines the root of the word(s) being defined. Greek and Hebrew words have roots or word ancestors that may enlighten the reader to understand and define the word. Greek and Hebrew are ancient languages that predate English. English words also have roots or ancestors that may have a relevance on determining meaning of the word. A reader can gain insight from the root words of these Bible words. There is a caution for the reader when looking at these roots, however, because the root may give some revelation about the word that can be a distraction from the actual meaning in the context.

In English, these words have interesting roots: gymnasium, infest, husband, fool, foreign, juggernaut, and psalm. "Gymnasium" means a place to exercise while the Greek root of the word means a place to exercise naked. The root carried meaning into the current definition, but not all of the meaning. The Greek word *gymnasio* is used in the New Testament in 1 Timothy 4:7, where Paul commands us "to exercise ourselves unto godliness." "Infest" means "to spread or swarm in or over," while the root is a Latin word meaning "hostile." The Latin root can add some understanding to the meaning but not carry all of it.

"Husband" is an interesting word meaning "the male participant in a marriage." The root of the word "husband" comes from two words combined. The first is Old English *hus*, meaning "house," and the second half of the word means to "dwell" or "inhabit." The etymology of "husband" means a husband is one who inhabits a house, connoting ownership. Your husband may sit on the couch all weekend watching sports and seem like someone inhabiting a house, true to the name husband! In the New Testament, the word translated "husband" is the normal word for "man" and the translation can only be determined by context. A unique word for the male participant in a marriage did not exist in Greek outside of a grammatical and syntactical package that caused the reader to understand that the word for male in this context meant a husband.

The English word "church" comes from a long line of Old English dialectical changes originating in the Greek language from the word *kyrios*, which is translated "Lord" in the New Testament. The root for "church" means that it means a place belonging to the Lord. The New Testament word for "church" is different. The Greek word is *ekklesia*, and its root means "called out ones."

The English word "psalm" is a transliteration of the Greek word "psalm." The root of the Greek word means "to pluck or strike," like you would a string of a harp or a string of an instrument. This means that psalms are by nature percussive. In our modern English, a psalm is not normally associated with percussion. Etymology is useful but not a complete, flawless tool to understand words.

USAGE

The third and best way to define a word is usage. The reader of the Bible must develop an interest in words, the meaning of words, and the usages of words. Words have a historical meaning that may shift over time. Words have ancestors and roots that expose some of the meaning without giving a complete picture. The way in which the word is used reveals the meaning of the word. Readers must examine the ways in which words are used to see their meaning.

English and the languages of the Bible, Greek, Hebrew, and Aramaic, differ in grammar and syntax. Words in the Bible do not always have cognates in English, and therefore some degree of meaning can be lost by translation. For example, the English word "love" is the translation of two different Greek words: *agape* and *philo*. English does not have multiple words for "love" like the Greek language does, so the reader is responsible for uncovering the depth of the original meaning from a translation that has some limitations.

EXAMPLES

Let us consider some specific examples of the importance of understanding words. The English word "again" is used to translate two different Greek words. The Bible used two Greek words translated "again." In John 3:3, Jesus told Nicodemus that he must be "born again." The two words translated "again" in English mean slightly different significant things. One means "again of the same kind," while the other means "again of a different kind." In John 3:3, Jesus used the word that means "again of a different kind." Nicodemus did not understand, and began to discuss being born again of the same kind from a mother's womb. Jesus continued the discourse and explained that one birth is of flesh from your mother and the second birth is of the Spirit of God into the family of God.

Another example is found in Exodus 20:7, where the Lord commands: "You shall not take the name of the Lord your God in vain, for the Lord will not hold him guiltless who takes the name of the Lord in vain" (NKJV). The word translated "take" is used more than 2000 times in the Hebrew Old Testament. The word does not mean "to speak." The word means "to carry," "to tote," or "to lift something up." It is used in tandem with speaking, like in Leviticus 9:9 when Aaron lifted up his hands and blessed the people. This conflation, physical lifting and carrying with the raising of the voice, did evolve into a usage that involved speaking and lifting your voice, but not during the period of Moses and before. In Exodus 20:7, God prohibited His children from carrying His name into a community, a place like Caanan, a school, or a workplace, for nothing. God's name should produce change. We go into a community in the name of the Lord. God will not hold you guiltless if you take the name of the Lord in vain. This commandment is a missionary commandment. God's name, if used and expressed properly, creates change among people.

In Matthew 16 and 18, Jesus used the word translated "church." The word translated church is *ekklesia*. The word is the combination of two words in the original language: *ek*, which means "out," which is where the word "exit" comes from; and *kaleo* which means "to call," which is where we get our word "call" from. The church, etymologically, means the "called out ones," and more specifically means the "called out assembly." In the Greek translation of the Hebrew Bible called the Septuagint (LXX), the word meant "assembly," or "gathering." The etymology of the word expresses to the reader that the church is called out of the world and separate to the Lord Jesus Christ. The English translators chose "church," which meant "belonging to the Lord," as the closest cognate that could be found.

The word church is used 108 times in the New Testament. The word is used in three ways and therefore defined in three ways. In 90% of the usages, the word "church" is used as a local body of baptized believers who have covenanted together to follow the doctrine and teaching of the Lord Jesus Christ (94 out of 108: Matthew 18:17, Acts 2:47, Acts 5:11, Acts 8:1, 3, 9:31, 13:1, 14:23, 14:27, 15:3, 22, 41, 16:5, 18:22, 20:17, 20:28, Romans 16:1, 3-5, 16, 23, 1 Cor. 1:2, 4:17, 6:4, 7:17, 10:32, 11:16, 11:18, 11:22, 12:27-28, 14:4-5, 14:12, 18-19, 27-28, 34-35, 16:1, 19, 2 Cor. 1:1, 8:1, 18-19, 23-24, 11:8, 12:13, Galatians 1:1-2, 1:21-22, Ephesians 1:1, Philippians 1:1, Colossians 1:1, 4:15-16, I Thess. 1:1, 2:14, II Thess. 1:1, 4, I Timothy 3:5, 14-15, 5:16, Philemon 1-2, James 5:14, III John 6, Revelation 1:4, 11, 20, 2:1, 7-8, 11, 12, 17, 18, 20, 23, 3:1, 6-7, 13-14, 22, 22:16, not an exhaustive list).

The second way the word "church" is used is institutional, (13 out of 108, Matt. 16: 18, 1 Cor. 15:9, Gal. 1:13, Eph. 1:22-23, 3:10, 3:21, 5:25, 29, 32, Col. 1: 18, 24, 27, Hebrews 12:22-24). The institutional usage does not refer to an undefined grouping. The word meant the collection of all the individual churches. In Ephesians 5, Paul wrote "Husbands, love your wives, just as Christ also loved the church and gave Himself for her." The husbands and the wives are a collection of all the husbands and all the wives, just as in this usage the church is a collection of all the local and visible churches.

Finally, the word "church" is used in a futuristic way, as a future gathering that is local and visible (1 out of 108). In Ephesians 5:27 it states, "That He might present her unto Himself a glorious church, not having spot or wrinkle or any such thing, but that she should be holy and without blemish." In all three usages, the word means a local and visible body. The futuristic church assembled in heaven will be local and visible.

One more example is the word "meek." In the Sermon on the Mount, the Lord Jesus states, "Blessed are the meek for they shall inherit the earth" (Matthew 5:5.) The word is also used in Matthew 21:5 and 1 Peter 3:4. The New American Standard version translated the word as "gentle". Wycliffe's translation is "a mild man." *Robertson's Word Pictures* states, "The ancients used the word for outward conduct and towards men. They did not rank it as a virtue anyhow. It was a mild equanimity that was sometimes negative and sometimes positively kind. But Jesus lifted the word to a nobility never attained before. In fact, the Beatitudes assume a new heart, for the natural man does not find in happiness the qualities mentioned here by Christ. The English word "meek" has largely lost the fine blend of spiritual poise and strength meant by the Master. He calls himself "meek and lowly in heart" (Matt. 11:29) and Moses is also called meek. It is the gentleness of strength, not mere effeminacy."[6] Meekness is strength under control. A horse that has been broken is a meek horse. The animal possesses great strength, but the strength is placed in the hand of the master to be used to serve the purpose of the master. Jesus called us to be strong but also meek, or easily controlled.

BAPTIZE

The word "baptize" deserves a more detailed explanation. It is a transliteration of the Greek word *baptizo*. The original translators of the English Bible refused to translate the word and simply brought the word into English as a loan word. The word is used in two major ways with four different usages in each one. The *Enhanced Strong's Concordance* defines *baptizo* as: "1) to dip repeatedly, to immerse, to submerge (of vessels sunk). 2) to cleanse by dipping or submerging, to wash, to make clean with water, to wash one's self, bathe. 3) to overwhelm."[7]

The clearest example that shows the meaning of *baptizo* from outside of Scripture is a text from the Greek poet and physician Nicander, who lived about 200 B.C. This text is a recipe for making pickles, and it is helpful because it uses two related words. Nicander

---

[6] Robertson, *Word Pictures in the New Testament*, 41.
[7] James Strong, Warren Patrick Baker, and Spiros Zodhiates, *AMG's Annotated Strong's Dictionaries* (Chattanooga, TN: AMG Publishers, 2009), 927.

says that to make a pickle, the vegetable should first be "dipped" (*bapto*) into boiling water and then "baptized" (*baptizo*) in a vinegar solution. Both verbs concern the immersing of vegetables in a solution. But the first is temporary. The second, the act of baptizing the vegetable, produces a permanent change. When used in the New Testament, this word more often refers to our union and identification with Christ than to our water baptism. For example in Mark 16:16 it states, "He that believes and is baptized shall be saved'. Christ is saying that mere intellectual assent is not enough. There must be a union with him, a real change, like the vegetable to the pickle![8]

Dr. Thomas J. Conant, in his *Meaning and Use of Baptizein*, sums up a study of the use of the word throughout the history of Greek literature, "The word *baptizein*, during the whole existence of the Greek as a spoken language, had a perfectly defined and unvarying import. In its literal use, it meant as has been shown to be put entirely into or under a liquid."[9] The words "sprinkling" and "pouring" are never used in the New Testament for the rite of baptism. This has compelled scholars of all denominational groups, including men such as Martin Luther and John Calvin, to admit that the original meaning and New Testament use of *baptizo* meant "immersion."[10]

The etymology of the word *baptizo* came from the word *bapto* which means "to dip in order to dye something." All the usages of the

---

[8] Anand Mahadevan, "What a Jar of Pickles Teaches Us About Baptism," *The Gospel Coalition*, September 16, 2022, https://in.thegospelcoalition.org/blogs/enjoy-the-gospel/baptism/.

[9] Thomas J. Conant, *The Meaning and Use of Baptizein* (New York: American Bible Union, 1868), 158-9.

[10] W. T. Beeby, *The Anabaptists of the 16th Century and the Baptists of the 19th Century* (London: G. Wightman, 1838).

word can be confusing. There are two distinct usages with four subcategories under each usage. The first is physical into water.

1) Immersion in water – Mark 7:4 & Luke 11:38. The word is used for washing by submerging. The word was used in the time of Hippocrates in the writings of Plato to mean to sink a ship. It was used in ancient writings figuratively for going under as well: to sink into a sleep or intoxication.

2) Physical believer's baptism – Mark 16:15-16, Hebrews 6:3, Mt. 28:19; Acts 2:38; 2:41; 8:12, 16, 36, 38; 9:18; 10:47-48; 16:15, 33; 18:8; 19:3, 5; 1 Cor. 1:14-16; 1 Peter 3:21; Eph. 4:5. This baptism is believer's baptism. Ephesians 4:4 speaks of the Spirit's work of uniting all in one body and one hope. 5:5 speaks to the baptism that is directly linked to the Son, believer's baptism. Believer's baptism is the outward sign of the one faith and one Lord.

3) The baptism of John the Baptist unto repentance – Mk. 1:4; Acts 13:24; To ceremonially cleanse and demonstrate purifying – (Mt 3:6; Mt 20:22 ; Mk 16:16); the one Baptizing (the Baptist), (Mk 6:14, 24) Hebrews 9:10; Mark 7:8. John's baptism was immersing into water to identify yourself with the ministry of John and to signify the repentance of sin and cleansing from sin that comes through repentance and confession (Matthew 3:6). Ceremonial washings were very common for Jews and Old Testament saints as images for purification and ritual. It appears that this baptism was more than once. It happened repeatedly to confess sins. This was ceremonial (or why else would Jesus have accepted it?). Jesus

was not a sinner, but to fulfill all righteousness He accepted a ceremonial cleansing although the only cleansing was through Himself (Acts 13: Acts 19; John 1:31).

4) The baptism of the dead – 1 Cor. 15:29. There are five different views among scholars as to what this means.

   a) Proxy baptism on behalf of dead people. This occurs when a person is baptized in the place of someone who has already died. Although there is no evidence of vicarious baptism in ancient Judaism, posthumous symbols could be employed. For instance, if someone was to be executed, Jewish teachers said that his death could atone for his sins; if he died before he could be executed, however, the people placed a stone on the coffin, symbolically enacting his stoning so that his execution would still count with God.

   b) Baptized to take the place of those who have already died. In this view, Paul would have mentioned baptism for the dead to illustrate how that the church believes in a resurrection. Why win anyone to Christ if there is no resurrection from the dead? Why baptize anyone for the people who have now died to replace the members of the church if there was no resurrection? They would live for Christ, but it would be in vain. Since there is not a direct sanction against this baptism this seems more plausible than the first or third options.

   c) For those who denied the resurrection, they just baptized people for the dead. Paul was speaking against the false teachers who believed that there was no resurrection. He used one of their own practices as an illustration that the resurrection was a part of the original worldview of Christianity and the faith.

d) Putting off the baptism until near death.

e) Those baptized on behalf of the testimony of some now dead people.

The second category of usage is spiritual or symbolic baptism. Jesus asked His disciples if they were able "to baptized with the baptism with which I am baptized?" (Mark 10:38).

1) Suffer severely – Mk 10:38, 39; Lk 12:50; Mt 20:22). This has been called the baptism of sin upon Christ at Calvary.

2) Spiritual baptism of the believer into Christ – Col. 2:12, Romans 6:3-4; Galatians 3:27.

3) Spiritual baptism of the Holy Spirit into believers at Pentecost as an enduement of power and subsequently upon conversion – Matthew 3:1, Mark 1:8, Luke 3:16, John 1:33, and Acts 1:5. Paul stated: "For in one Spirit we were all baptized into one body–Jews or Greeks, slaves or free–and all were made to drink of one Spirit" (1 Corinthians 12:13).

Three passages give commentary on the events at Pentecost as an enabling of the Holy Spirit rather than an indwelling for salvation: Luke 24:49, "endued with power;" Acts 10:44-48, "fell upon those;" "gift of the Holy Spirit;" Acts 11:15, "Holy Spirit fell upon them."

4) The baptism of Israel into Moses – 1 Cor. 10:2. Identifying the children of Israel with Moses, their leader.

WORDS TRANSLATED "HELL"

1) *Sheol* – The Hebrew word *Sheol* is used 64 times in the Old Testament. The King James Version translated it 31 times as "grave," thirty times as "Hell," and three times as "pit." *Sheol* is from the root word meaning "to ask" or "demand," meaning an insatiable demand for more. Proverbs 27:2 states, "Hell and destruction are never full." Genesis 37:35 and Numbers 16:30 demonstrate how that both good and bad men go there. Genesis 37:35, "All his sons and all his daughters rose up to comfort him, but he refused to be comforted and said, 'No, I shall go down to Sheol to my son, mourning.' Thus his father wept for him." Numbers 16:30, "But if the Lord creates something new, and the ground opens its mouth and swallows them up with all that belongs to them, and they go down alive into Sheol, then you shall know that these men have despised the Lord."

   The English Standard Version translates the word in some texts and transliterates the word, *Sheol*, in some texts, such as the previous two examples. The word is elastic enough to mean "the grave" and "the eternal state of the soul" without specifying heaven or hell. The word can mean "underworld," which connotes grave, hell, or the abode of the dead.

2) *Hades* – The Greek word is used 11 times in the New Testament. The *Zondervan Pictorial Encyclopedia* states that according to Homer, *Hades* was the name of the underworld and the Greek god of the underworld, also known as Pluto. The word's etymology is thought to be from the word "to

see," with the negation as a prefix, "the unseen." The Greek word *Hades* was used to translate several Hebrew words in the Greek translation of the Hebrew Bible (also known as the Septuagint or LXX), namely, "the pit," "stillness," "death," "those who bring death," "deep darkness," and, most commonly, "Sheol." Used as the abode of the dead in the New Testament, but the majority of the 10 usages relate to the place of everlasting torment for the damned (Acts 2:27 translates Sheol and means abode of the dead, but Luke 16:23 means the place of torment). Jesus said that the gates of *Hades* will not prevail against the church. Four times in the book of Revelation, John used *Hades*, including the words of Jesus saying that He possesses "the keys of death and Hades." Peter used the word twice in the great sermon at Pentecost, quoting Psalm 16:10 and applying it. Jesus used *Hades* to say that the rich man, in Luke 16, died and went to *Hades*.[11]

3) *Gehenna* was used in the Hebrew Scriptures in 2 Kings 23:10, 2 Ch. 28:3; 33:6; Je. 7:31; 32:35, and means "hell," or "hellfire." The word is derived from Hebrew *ge-hinnom*, meaning "valley of Hinnom," also known as "the valley of the son(s) of Hinnom."[12] Located west and south of Jerusalem and running into the Kidron Valley at a point opposite the modern village of Silwan or Siloam, the valley of Hinnom once formed part of the boundary between the tribes of Judah and Benjamin (Josh.

[11] H. Buis, "Hades," in *The Zondervan Encyclopedia of the Bible*, vol. 3, ed. Merrill C. Tenney (Grand Rapids: Zondervan, 1976), 7.
[12] Werner E. Lemke, "Gehenna," in *The HarperCollins Bible Dictionary*, eds. P. J. Achtemeier, et al. (New York: HarperCollins Publishers, 1996), 335.

15:8; 18:16; Neh. 11:30).[13] During the monarchical period, it became the site of an infamous high place (called 'Topheth' and derived from an Aramaic word meaning 'fireplace'), where some of the kings of Judah engaged in forbidden religious practices, including human sacrifice by fire (2 Chron. 28:3; 33:6; Jer. 7:31; 32:35).[14] Because of this, Jeremiah spoke of its impending judgment and destruction (Jer. 7:32; 19:6). King Josiah put an end to these practices by destroying the high place in the valley of Hinnom (2 Kings 23:10).[15] Because of these associations with fiery destruction and judgment, the word *Gehenna* came to be used metaphorically during the intertestamental period as a designation for hell or eternal damnation. In the New Testament, the word is used only in this way and never as a geographic place name. As such, *Gehenna* is to be distinguished from *Hades*, which is either the abode of all the dead in general (Acts 2:27, 31; Rev. 20:13-14) or the place where the wicked await the final judgment. By contrast, the righteous enter paradise, or a state of bliss, immediately upon death (Luke 16:19-31; 23:43; 2 Cor. 12:3). Jesus exclusively used a term translated "Hell" in the New Testament. Jesus warned his disciples of committing sins that would lead to *Gehenna* (Matt. 5:22, 29-30; 23:33; Mark 9:45; Luke 12:5). In the New Testament, *Gehenna* designated the

---

[13] C. Mark McCormick, "Valley of Hinnom," in *The New Interpreter's Dictionary of the Bible D-H*, eds. K. D. Sakenfeld, et al. (Nashville: Abingdon, 2007), 826.

[14] "Tophet," in *The Holman Bible Dictionary*, ed. Trent C. Butler, et al. (Nashville: Holman, 1991), 1357.

[15] H. Buis, "Hades," in *The Zondervan Encyclopedia of the Bible*, vol. 3, ed. Merrill C. Tenney (Grand Rapids: Zondervan, 1976), 7.

place or state of the final punishment of the wicked. It is variously described as a fiery furnace (Matt. 13:42, 50), an unquenchable fire (Mark 9:43), or an eternal fire prepared for the devil and his angels (Matt. 25:41).

4) *Tartarus* appears in 2 Peter 2:4. *Thayer's Greek-English Lexicon of the New Testament* states, "The name of a subterranean region, doleful and dark, regarded by the ancient Greeks as the abode of the wicked dead, where they suffer punishment for their evil deeds; it answers to Gehenna of the Jews."[16] The Greeks used this word and Peter then used it in 2 Peter to express Hell to his audience.

VERBS

Verbs contain the action in the passages of Holy Scripture. Verbs xpose meaning to the reader. The original languages use verbs in a different way than English. For example, Hebrew has seven grammatical constructions for verbs to reveal the active or passive voice and the cause of the action. In Exodus 3:7, the Lord spoke to Moses from the burning bush saying, "I have surely seen the affliction of my people." Other translations say, "indeed seen the affliction" (NIV). This statement contains two verb forms combined, which results in a strong way for God to say that I have been caused to see. The implication is that Moses implied that God had not seen because He had not acted. The Lord rebutted that notion with the verb formation. The English translations capture it with the words "surely"

---

[16]Joseph H. Thayer, *Thayer's Greek-English Lexicon of the New Testament* (Peabody, MA: Hendrickson, 1996), 615.

or "indeed." God sees. God hears our cries. God knows and does not forget.

Greek verbs have voice, mood, tense, person, and number. These complexities are simplified by the translations and rendered into English. The complexities explain the variety of translations. Some translations seek to translated word for word, such as the New American Standard (NASB), while others seek to translate phrase to phrase, like the New International Version (NIV), without retaining as much specificity. Other translations will straddle these two poles to make the English readable while maintaining much of the complexity of the verbs.

Voice means that a verb form is active, passive, or middle. An active verb means that the subject performs the action, "I preached the gospel." The passive voice means that the action is being performed to or on the subject, "I was filled by the Spirit." The middle voice is used when the subject performs the action on themselves, "I humbled myself." The verb's mood does not speak of some verbs are cranky or snarky. Mood means indicative, subjunctive (which uses "may" as a helping word, infinitival (which uses "to" as helping word, participial (which ends in "ing"), or imperative. Each mood clarifies the verbs and conveys a different meaning.

Tense means that a verb is present, past or aorist, future, perfect, or future perfect. Tense impacts Matthew 16:19 when Jesus said that "whatever you bind on earth will have already been bound in heaven." The tense of the first verb translated "will have" is future middle, and the tense of the second verb translated "been bound" is a perfect passive. Whatever you bind on earth will have already been bound in heaven. The perfect passive says that the binding has already occurred and is completed, and the future middle says that we will see it in the future. Therefore, as we bind the gospel on the earth, which is the keys of the kingdom, then the gospel will have been bound in heaven, but if we loose the gospel on the earth then the gospel will have already been loosed in heaven. When the gospel is preached, then people will be saved.

THE NAME OF THE LORD

In Hebrew, two distinct words are translated with the four letters l-o-r-d. One word used is the divine name translated and appearing as LORD, often referred to as Yahweh. A second word used is a title translated "Lord," known as Adoniah. LORD was also translated by the KJV as "Jehovah" seven times. Hebrew words do not have vowels in the original manuscripts because vowel pointing was not invented by the Masoretes until Hebrew began to disappear as a spoken language in the eighth century AD. Therefore, nobody really knows how to pronounce the divine name. When the translators of the King James Version translated the name, on seven occasions they took the four consonants from the Masoretic text that were known and combined them with the vowels of Adoniah to make the word Jehovah. This has caused confusion and aided the cult of Jehovah's Witness and the Watchtower Society to claim special hidden revelation.

The two words, LORD and Lord, are used in the same passage on many occasions. For example, Isaiah 6:1 says, "I saw the Lord sitting upon a throne. . ." and Isaiah 6:3 says, "Holy, holy, holy is the LORD of hosts: the whole earth is full of his glory." The divine name, LORD, is derived from the verb "to exist" as the Lord explained to Moses in Exodus 3. The Lord instructed Moses to tell Pharoah and the people that "I am that I am" has sent you. This name spoke of the self-existent nature of the LORD. Adoniah comes from an unknown root but means "the ruler, master, or sovereign."

American English rarely uses "Lord" outside of a religious context. The exceptions seem to be "drug lord" or "landlord." The Hebrew word *Adonai* was used often to be the title of an exalted position. The divine name was not used by the Hebrews for fear and reverence of it. It is believed that when scribes wrote the divine name, they would use a different instrument for each letter to preserve the holiness of the name. The divine name appeared more that 6800 times in the Hebrew Old Testament.

Most if not all English Bible translations contain an introduction that explains the treatment of these words used for God when they appear by themselves or coupled with other words used for God. The reader would benefit from reading the translator's words concerning their approach.

A Few Cautions for the Reader

Modern tools, artificial intelligence, and the proliferation of Bible interpreters online have made Bible research accessible to the average reader. I started seminary in 1993 when you had to go to a reference room in a library with expensive, old, large books written by scholars to learn about words. These processes were time consuming and challenging. At this moment, most of that material is available in a

Google search. However, it is perilous to assume that every source is trustworthy and that conclusions are accurate and ready to present as truth. A few boundaries are needed for the spiritual health of the reader and the health of the church.

First, a word only has one meaning in any given text. Words mean different things depending upon the context. "Cool" can mean temperature or a person's style and disposition. "Red" can mean stop or angry depending on the context. You will find words that are used in various ways, and in each usage the word will mean one thing.

Second, the reader must not build doctrines around one word. Cults thrive in the environment of unwise interpreters who are led astray from the orthodox truth by the unusual interpretation of one or two words. Factions split churches over one or two voices captured by foolish disputes over a few words in Scripture. Paul warned against this in Titus 3.

Third, God gifted you with the Bible, the Holy Spirit, and pastors or elders to help you. The reader should consult their spiritual leaders before adopting a new position. I suggest that you ask your pastor: "Am I correct to conclude from this study . . . ?" The journey of discovering the Bible is not to be a solitary undertaking. God has placed wise saints who exceed your maturity to assist you.

Fourth, clear texts should interpret unclear texts. I was debating a member of the Church of Latter-Day Saints, a Mormon, on one occasion. I asked him to show me the Scripture, either Old or New Testament, that prophesied that Jesus would not be the full and final revelation and that an authentic Christian would be looking for the full revelation at a much later time (according to them the nineteenth century when Joseph Smith received the tablets from Moroniah). The zealous Mormon claimed that the prophesies concerning the coming Comforter applied to Joseph Smith. I refuted the argument by saying that those texts, without question, spoke of the day of Pentecost and the work of the Holy Spirit, and that the faith was once for all delivered to the saints of the first century. He then pointed to an obscure text in Ezekiel to attempt to say that the New Testament would need a companion volume called the Book of Mormon for the full revelation to be known. The text spoke of two sticks coming together and he claimed that this prefigured the Book of Mormon. The tragic reality remains that unstable men and women pervert the Scriptures through unsound interpretations to the end that lives would be destroyed by false teaching. The Bible contains a unity of message, and the reader must allow the clear texts to interpret the unclear texts.

Chapter 6
GENRE

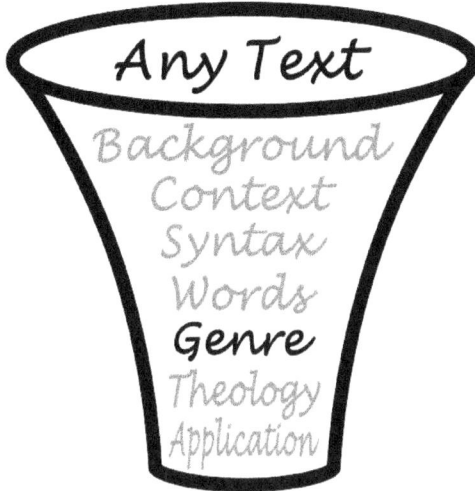

The Bible contains 66 books from approximately forty different authors from three continents, written over the course of 1500 years. The greatest book ever written is 66 different books with many different genres or types of writing: poems, narrative history, prophesy, hyperbole, apocalyptic, metaphors, allegories, similes, genealogies, parables, an epic, psalms, acrostics, chiasms, epistles, and histories. Every genre possesses a different style, a different common written form, and a different method of meaning.

In the current setting, jokes have different styles and rules. Political speeches or songs or sermons or coaches' rants are different genres of communication. The audience, the moment, the style of presentation, and the method of understanding changes. In March of

2022, Will Smith publicly slapped Chris Rock at the Academy Awards because Chris Rock said something about Smith's wife in a joke. The Academy of Motion Picture Arts and Sciences, The Screen Actors Guild-American Federation of Television and Radio Artists, and many Hollywood figures condemned Will Smith. Some defended Smith, saying that a joke about his wife's medical condition and shaved head was over the top. One actress said: "It was a joke." Jokes give the speaker access to words not normally used, irregular content, because they are a different type of communication.

In the Bible, different genres allow the speaker to say things that would not be the normal words to move the listener. Jesus called a Syrophoenician women a dog (Mark 7:26-28) for effect. The psalmist used imprecatory language for effect, acceptable and understood inside the genre. The Gospel writers record the Lord Jesus using hyperbole to make points to His audience. Jesus commanded them to pluck their eyes out or cut their hands off if they caused them to sin. Jesus told them to hate their mother and their father. Each author wrote in a genre-specific way. The reader must be able to recognize the uniqueness and the shifts. The shifts are not easy to see as Grant Osborne recognized in *The Hermeneutical Spiral*, "The modern reader needs help in understanding how those ancient genres functioned."[17]

Osborne explained genre analysis as a set of literary conventions or norms shared by readers and writers. He explained, "Genre analysis represents both large and small portions of Scripture (entire books) and smaller units. Poetry can be found in the Psalms, but it is also a subgenre found in both wisdom and prophetic literature. This is also

---

[17] Osborne, *The Hermeneutical Spiral*, 182.

true in the New Testament. Parable is a subgenre only, but it is so critical to the teaching of Jesus that we must treat it separately."[18] Communication involves genre and the understanding of it.

THE LAW

The law presented unique interpretive challenges because of the nature of the genre. The law was delivered in three forms: moral law, civil law, and ceremonial law. These laws were combined in the first five books of the Bible, particularly Exodus, Leviticus, Numbers, and Deuteronomy.

The moral law, summarized succinctly in the Ten Commandments, issued commands that transcend time and culture, containing prohibitions against lying, coveting, murder, stealing, idolatry, the mishandling of the name of the Lord, and dishonoring parents. Jesus was asked to summarize the law, and He did on several occasions. He stated, "Love the Lord your God with all your heart, your soul, and your mind and to love your neighbor as yourself."

The civil law revealed God's will for the theocracy of Israel to interpret and enforce these moral laws among a hard-hearted people. God hates divorce but allows it. God hates slavery but gives a context to address it legally and bring an end to it. The Lord did not want Israel to have a monarchy, a king. Yet, in the civil law in Deuteronomy 17, the Lord gave prescriptive commands to the future monarchy. The civil law contains enforcement procedures that bear witness to the essence of the moral law but do not become the enforcement mechanisms in every time and culture. All punishments of behavior

---

[18] Osborne, *The Hermeneutical Spiral*, 182.

came from a civil perspective. God prescribed the way in which the theocracy under Moses should function, organized by families and the head of the household who basically administered justice until the Law of Moses was established, and then the issues came before the tribal leaders and to Moses. God spoke of capital punishment by stoning, levying fines, requiring repayment, and an entire system around the concept of retributive justice, an eye for an eye and a tooth for a tooth. God spoke of a justified war against another clan or nation or city.

The ceremonial law was given for the priests and the people to clarify the expectations of worship, the prescribed approach to worship, and the system to sustain worship throughout the future of the Hebrew people. The ceremonial system gave the Hebrews pilgrimage schedules, dietary laws, dress codes, ritualistic process, and a holistic cultural set of practices consistent with the moral and civil laws.

The law confused the Hebrew people. Their scribes and teachers debated about hand washing procedures, Sabbath regulations, marriage and divorce, and treatment of family and neighbors. Jesus attacked these subjects in the Sermon on the Mount, addressing the confusion around the law. He said: "You have heard it said an eye for an eye and a tooth for a tooth, but I say unto you." Jesus shared a parable, the parable of the Good Samaritan, to answer the debate about defining who a neighbor to the Jew was. He shocked them by making the Samaritan the hero of the story and the priests the lawbreakers of the story. Jesus called his audience to recognize occasions when the ceremonial law was not followed because of a higher law demanding a different action.

Peter and the early church struggled with understanding the interpretation of the law. Peter refused to eat with Gentiles in Galatians 2 and the Apostle Paul rebuked him. Peter refused to eat the unkosher foods that the Lord provided and was rebuked by a voice from heaven, "What God has made clean, do not call common" (Acts 11:9). The ceremonial law was fulfilled in Christ. No distinction between Jew and Gentile could be made according to the Lord because of the finished work of Christ. The civil law was the moral law interpreted in the context of a hard-hearted, rebellious people. The moral law transcends any culture, with authority prescribing that which is morally pure and righteous.

SIMILES, METAPHORS, PARABLES, AND ALLEGORIES

A simile is a comparison using "like" or "as." In Matthew 23:27-28, Jesus rebuked the Pharisees and religious leaders with a simile, "Woe to you, scribes and Pharisees, hypocrites! For you are like whitewashed tombs, which outwardly appear beautiful, but within are full of dead people's bones and all uncleanness. So you also outwardly appear righteous to others, but within you are full of hypocrisy and lawlessness."

A parable extends the simile to express and explain the comparison fully. The story and the application are distinct from each other. A parable has one focus for comparison and therefore one meaning. The Old Testament and the New Testament contains parables such as the parable of Luke 15 or the parable of the vineyard in Isaiah 5:1-7. Jesus spoke a thorough explanation of parables at the beginning of His preaching ministry. His initial parable was the parable of the sower, recorded in Matthew 13:1-23, Mark 4:1-20, and Luke 8:4-15. This extended comparison of a sower and the gospel preacher served as a guide to the process of spreading the good news and the results that the gospel brings among a people. Jesus highlighted the soil, or the heart of the hearer, as the determining factor for response to the seed. The sower, the seed, the simplicity of the process, the insignificance of the message depicted in a small seed, the weather, and the capability of the seed remain the same. The soil determined that growth of the seed. The parable focused the hearer on having a prepared heart for the sown seed. Jesus portrayed the enemy of the seed in the parable.

Jesus used parables to reveal and conceal the truth in a persecuted environment. He exposed leaders without severe offense, without speaking plain language, and with vivid clarity and simplicity. Jesus made His message memorable and contextual through these stories to a non-literate audience. The Bible says that the common man heard Him gladly. Jesus often explained the parables in private to the disciples so that the secrets of the kingdom could be given to them, but to everyone on the outside He spoke in parables.

The reader must look for the single point of comparison that carries the interpretive weight. In Luke 15, Jesus told the grumbling Pharisees and scribes "this parable." The reader may be tempted to interpret Luke 15 as three parables (the lost sheep, the lost coin, and the lost son) but Jesus stated that one parable is in the text. The one parable has three scenes with the same plot line: something cherished is lost, something cherished is found, and a justified, moral celebration ensues upon finding that which was lost. The parable focused upon the experience of the Father finding lost people and recovering them. The scribes and Pharisees grumbled because Jesus received and ate with sinners. The joy in heaven and the joy of Jesus was justified, "It was fitting to celebrate and be glad" (Luke 15:32).

Metaphors are comparisons that do not use "like" or "as," and allegories are extended metaphors. In John 15:1 Jesus said that I am the vine, and you are the branches. This passage is an extended metaphor or an allegory. Allegories have multiple points of comparison unlike the parable which tends to have one. Few passages are allegories in the Bible.

APOCALYPTIC

Originating in the Greek word *apokalupsis,* which means uncovering, apocalyptic writing focuses on revealing what has been hidden regarding future events the end times. It is highly symbolic, with the goal of prediction and comfort through the purpose of God through time. These texts had meaning when they were written. These texts continue to have meaning today, revealing ongoing events and signs of the times. Apocalyptic material was recorded in Daniel, Isaiah, Revelation, Ezekiel, and Zechariah.

Daniel wrote predictive material concerning the future of the kingdoms of the world, the coming Messiah, the Jewish people, and the last days. His writing possessed deep symbolism, while maintaining a literal interpretation for prediction. The Lord gave him visions of events to come. For the reader, Daniel serves as a "how to" guide to understanding other apocalyptic material. Isaiah and Ezekiel used symbolic language to speak of the nature and person of God, future events, and the current realities facing their audience. Zechariah and John in the Revelation wrote with inspired symbolism to comfort the people in their audience and to reveal future events to the people of God to come.

Pastors and scholars have differed on interpreting the Book of Revelation. Four different views have emerged on Revelation: preterist, historicist, idealist, and futurist. The preterist believes that Revelation was written for the era of the author and the events recorded are now in our past, fulfilled in the first or second century. The historicist believes that Revelation discloses a complete panorama of the future of the church from the first century until the last day. The idealist, like early church Alexandrian fathers Clement and Origin, believes that the book contains a timeless-symbolic approach of future events in order to comfort and display the greatness of our God. Futurists take the book of Revelation like Daniel, looking for prophetic fulfillment, future events foretold in symbols, and literal unveiling of the future.

The view that the reader takes to the material will determine their view on the future unveiling of the reign of Christ. The preterist and the idealist believe in a symbolic millennial reign and are therefore amillennialist, looking for the return of Christ without concern for a millennium. The futurist believes in a literal 1000-year reign and could be pre-millennial or post-millennial, looking for the return of Christ before the 1000-year reign on earth or after the 1000-year reign on earth.

PROPHECY

The Old Testament prophets spoke from God as they were moved by the Spirit of God. They searched and inquired carefully as to the One who was to come, the time of His coming, and the complete and final restoration of the kingdom to God's people, Israel. The prophets include writers and non-writers. Isaiah, Micah, Nahum, Zechariah, Daniel, Hosea, Joel, Amos, Obediah, Malachi, Haggai, Jeremiah, Ezekiel, Habbakkuk, Zephaniah, and Jonah wrote timeless books that couched into the milieu and moment of their generation. Elijah, Elisha, and Nathan preached but did not write their prophecies. They are recorded in the historical books of the Old Testament.

The prophets wrote for three purposes. First, their prophecies predicted future events. Isaiah 6, 7, 8, 9, 40, 42, 49, 50, and 53 chronicled the life, death, and resurrection of the suffering servant who was to come. Micah 5:2 recorded the birthplace and nature of this soon coming King. Zechariah explained that He would arrive on a donkey colt into Jerusalem as the King. The prophets not only wrote of the coming of the Messiah but also concerning the future of the nation, of kings, of cities, and of the world.

Second, their prophecies revealed concealed facts about their present. Daniel famously explained the writing on the wall hours before the King would be killed and his kingdom would be given to the Medes and the Persians. Amos exposed the future of the King of

Israel and his kingdom by prophesying that the King's wife would be a harlot in the city and the nation would be led away captive.

Third, their prophecies dispensed instruction, comfort, and exhortation in powerful, impassioned language. Isaiah would plead with the people to come and reason together to seek cleansing and forgiveness. Micah called upon the nations to turn from their wickedness. Elijah and Elisha wrestled with the dark corrupt vile Ahab and Jezebel in a fruitless effort to turn them from their wickedness. Nathan exposed and confronted David in his sin with Bathsheba and Uriah the Hittite. Haggai rebuked the people of God from neglecting the Temple to build their own paneled houses. Malachi asked the people if a man could rob God. He shined the light of God's revelation upon their wicked practices intended to deceive and manipulate God.

The prophets' revelations are contained in rich prose, parallelisms, parables, allegories, and unique declarations. A skilled reader can discover the elegance and the force of these heart-rending messages.

PROVERBS

The book of Proverbs contains 915 verses. This book is the recorded wisdom of Solomon. Proverbs may be defined, according to Osborne, as brief statements of universally accepted truth in such a way as to make it memorable.[19] A proverb is a general statement generally applied that brings general results. The beauty of a proverb appears in its truth wrapped in a memorable package. The danger of a proverb becomes apparent when a proverb is stretched to become a promise. A proverb exposes people, human behavior, and general truth about

[19] Osborne, *The Hermeneutical Spiral*, 247.

it. A proverb is not a guarantee or an infallible predictor of behavior. These lessons involve general advice, not rigid codes.

The Proverbs can be misused to make a parent feel guilty if a child grows up and goes away from the Lord. The Proverbs can be misused to think that corporal punishment can change the bent or the rebellious nature of a young person. The rod of correction can drive rebellion from being expressed through severe consequences but not remove it from the heart. The Proverbs exhort the son to obey the parents because obedience is wisdom. Generally, this is true, but not in every case. These amazing principles are proverbs meant to enlighten the reader of the behavior and activities of humans as they encounter wisdom. The reader should enjoy them as intended.

NARRATIVE

Narrative texts of the Bible include at least half of the Scripture: Genesis, Exodus, Leviticus, Numbers, Deuteronomy, Job, Joshua, Judges, Ruth, 1 & 2 Samuel, 1 & 2 Kings, 1 & 2 Chronicles, Jonah, Ezra, Nehemiah, Esther, Matthew, Mark, Luke, John and Acts of the Apostles. The authors recorded theological history in narrative form. They wrote history with a purpose and the purpose dictated what was reported and recorded. Events were recorded without interpretation, simply reported. The purpose of the writing was stated outright in the case of the Gospel of John, "Now Jesus did many other signs in the presence of the disciples, which are not written in this book; but these are written so that you may believe that Jesus is the Christ, the Son of God, and that by believing you may have life in his name" (John 20:30-31).

In the Gospels, miracles functioned as enacted parables, and parables functioned as instructional miracles. In Mark 6:52, Mark recorded the miracle of feeding the five thousand and the walking on the water. As the narrative concerning walking on the water concluded, Mark wrote: "And he got into the boat with them, and the wind ceased. And they were utterly astounded, for they did not understand about the loaves, but their hearts were hardened" (Mark 6:51-52). The miracle performed by Jesus was intended to instruct the disciples, like a parable, and yet the disciples did not receive the instruction. Parables were recorded in various orders in the Synoptic Gospels to fit the intended purpose of the writer and to present the flow of revelation as received. Jesus was likely to have shared these parables on more than one occasion.

Structures, macro-structures, historical flow, items reported, plot, tension, character development, and dialogue organize these narratives to produce a unique style of history. Each book contributed to the flow of history centered around the coming Christ, the sustaining of the ancestral line of the promised seed of Abraham, the ministry of Christ, and the acts of the apostles to spread the gospel. The writers' purposes can be seen by the structures and macrostructures. Ruth, Jonah, Ezra, and Daniel evidence a macro-structure with intention as organization for the material.

Job, Genesis, Exodus, Leviticus, and Numbers display structures that place emphasis on the center of the books. Each center displays the Messiah in a unique way: the Redeemer that lives and will stand upon the earth, Abraham offering Isaac on Mt. Moriah, the Passover, the Day of Atonement, and the bronze serpent lifted in the wilderness.

Some narrative text placement demonstrates the writer's intentionality, such as the historical interlude in the book of Isaiah. Isaiah used the experience of a suffering king, Hezekiah, who brought deliverance to the people of God as symbol of the work of the Christ who was to come into history. First and Second Samuel recorded characters that carried the name of the Lord in a positive way and a negative way to display honor as a theme while explaining the Davidic covenant relationship. First and Second Kings gave a historical treatment of events in the divided kingdom, and 1 and 2 Chronicles recorded the spiritual events that moved history during the same time period. Luke organized his narrative in the Gospel of Luke to speak to a wealthy, powerful man. Therefore, he included parables unique to his gospel that spoke to the wealthy and powerful, events like the rich man and Lazarus, Zaccheaus, and Joseph of Arimathea. Mark was written for the Gentile and started with the ministry of Jesus instead of his family background. Acts followed the ministry of Peter and then Paul.

Some narrative texts serve as types of Christ. The Passover Lamb is a type of Christ referred to in the New Testament as a picture of the coming Messiah's sacrifice for us. The Temple was a type of Christ per the words of Jesus. Other texts lend themselves to comparison but fail to have the New Testament backing, like Joseph. The reader should be free to find illustrations but cautious to conclude that every comparison was the intention of the writer.

Chapter 7
THEOLOGY

Any Text

Background
Context
Syntax
Words
Genre
Theology
Application

Every text relates to the broader revelation found throughout the Bible. Therefore, the reader must allow the rest of the Bible to clarify, simplify, and certify meaning in any given text. The reader must ask and answer, "What does the rest of the Bible say about this text, the truths contained, and the subjects addressed?" These comparisons from one text to another produce a theology on any given subject.

SYSTEMATIC THEOLOGY

Comparing texts from different books and different chapters within the same book produces a teaching or a doctrine that is consistent throughout the Bible. The Bible has a unified message on subjects. For example, Paul instructed the readers in Ephesus that in an unsaved condition a person is dead in their trespasses and sins (Ephesians 2:1). Paul told the Romans that "all have sinned and come short of the glory of God" (Romans 3:23). In Romans 3:10, he explained that no person is righteous, no not one. David taught in the Psalm 51 that everyone was fashioned in the womb in iniquity and "in sin did my mother conceive me" (Psalm 51:5). Isaiah wrote that the sins that people commit separate them from God (Isaiah 59:2). Comparing the teaching of these texts creates a theology, or teaching, concerning the spiritual sinfulness of man. Man is not inherently good or moral. Man expresses his true nature in his behavior, and every person does that which is wrong. Therefore, every person is a sinner, an evil doer, separated from God because of their sin, and in need of a Savior. Jesus said that there is none good but one, and that one is God (Mark 10:18). The collective weight of these various texts creates a theology of sin in mankind. Every text studied has subjects and doctrines that the reading must put into the broader context of the rest of the Bible.

The teaching of the Bible concerning Jesus may be the most important theological subject revealed in the Bible. John explained the unique person of Jesus in his gospel. John referred to Jesus as the Word, "In the beginning was the Word and the Word was with God and the Word was God" (John 1:1). Jesus existed in the beginning. He had no beginning. He dwells outside of time and is coequal with God the Father. John further explained in verse 14, "And the Word became flesh and dwelt among us, and we beheld His glory as of the glory of the only-begotten of the Father, full of grace and truth." John taught that Jesus was eternal God, one with the Father in the beginning and separate from the Father for He was with God, the one who took on flesh while continuing to be God. He was God who became the God-man.

Paul taught the same thing with different words in Colossians 1:15, "He is the image of the invisible God." Jesus is God made visible. God is invisible, as John said in John 4:24, "God is spirit." Paul continued in Colossians 1:19 by saying that "it pleased the Father that in Him all the fulness should dwell." Jesus was not mostly or partially God. Jesus was all the fullness of God in bodily form. He was 100% God. Paul wrote in Colossians 2:9, "in Him dwells all the fulness of the Godhead bodily."

The writer of Hebrews echoed the same teaching, or doctrine, of the incarnation of God in Jesus. In Hebrews 1:3, speaking of Jesus, the writer stated, "who being the brightness of His glory and the express image of His person." Jesus is the person and glory of God existing in human form. Jesus was and is God. Many other texts can be studied that emphasize and support this glorious doctrine. Bible readers need to compare texts to gain clarity and support for the theology built by any one text.

These compared teachings are called doctrines or theology. Systematic theology organizes these teachings under subjects such as the doctrine of God, the doctrine of sin, the doctrine of the Holy Spirit, the doctrine of Jesus Christ, the doctrine of salvation, the doctrine of the second coming, and the doctrine of humanity. The reader should purchase a concise systematic theology as a reference to assist in studying the Bible. The Baptist Faith and Message 2000 is also available online, providing a wonderful summary of Bible doctrine and accompanying Scripture that support these beliefs.

CONFLICTING TEXTS

The Bible does, on rare occasions, present seemingly conflicting passages that need to be reconciled or synthesized through wise interpretation. Gospel or narrative accounts may contain different details about the same event. These accounts present little challenge when you understand that the different accounts are independent and from varying perspectives. Each writer did not record everything that occurred.

Other texts may contain more complicated challenges. For example, Paul and James appeared to make directly contradictory statements concerning faith and good works. Paul explained in Galatians 2 that a person is justified (declared righteous before God) by faith alone, "knowing that a man is not justified by the works of the law but by faith in Jesus Christ, even we have believed in Christ Jesus, that we might be justified by faith in Christ and not by the works of the law; for by the works of the law no flesh shall be justified" (Galatians 2:16). Paul continued, clarifying and emphasizing the teaching of justification by faith in Galatians 3:5-9, "Therefore He who supplies the Spirit to you and works miracles among you, does He do it by the works of the law, or by the hearing of faith? – just as Abraham believed God, and it was accounted to him for righteousness.' Therefore know that only those who are of faith are sons of Abraham. And the Scripture, foreseeing that God would justify the Gentiles by faith, preached the gospel to Abraham beforehand, saying, 'In you all the nations shall be blessed.' So then those who are of faith are blessed with believing Abraham."

James declared what might appear to be a direct contradiction to Paul's teaching concerning justification in James 2:21-24, "Was not Abraham our father justified by works when he offered Isaac his son on the altar? Do you see that faith was working together with his works, and by works faith was made perfect? And the Scripture was fulfilled which says, 'Abraham believed God, and it was accounted to him for righteousness.' And he was called the friend of God. You see then that a man is justified by works, and not by faith only." James announced that works and faith are both necessary to bring justification. Paul adamantly argued that faith alone was how justification is conveyed to the sinner. Martin Luther took such offense to the words of James that he diminished the contribution of the book in the greater content of the Bible. He called the book of James "the epistle of straw." How does a reader reconcile these seemingly conflicting texts?

Paul and James are not contradicting each other but complementing each other. Paul focuses on the root of good works, which is faith. He separated faith from works as does the Genesis account of Abraham's sacrifice and ultimate justification. Abraham was justified by faith. He presented the sacrifice by faith. Righteousness was imputed to Abraham through faith. Paul looked at the root of works and not the fruit of authentic faith, which is good works. James had been exposed to saying faith instead of saving faith. Saying faith merely professed trust in Christ without demonstrating that trust through fruit bearing and good works. James took exception with any concept that separated faith from good works. James called faith without works dead. Paul focused on the root and James focused on the fruit of genuine faith. In order to synthesize the two teachings, a simple statement will suffice: the faith that saves is a faith that works. Faith that does not work is disingenuous and dead. Works do not compete with faith, but works do accompany genuine faith. Paul claimed in Ephesians 2:8-10 that salvation comes by grace through faith, not of works, but unto good works, in which we should walk.

Narrative texts may also contain what might appear to be blatant conflicts. The census ordered by David in 2 Samuel 24:1 is explained by the writer of 2 Samuel in this way, "Again the anger of the Lord was aroused against Israel, and He moved David against them to say, "Go, number Israel and Judah." However, the writer of 1 Chronicles 21:1 explained the events in a very different manner, "Now Satan stood up against Israel, and moved David to number Israel." Could there be a more conflicting set of reports on this event? One account stated that the Lord moved David because He was angry while the other account explained that it was Satan that moved David. Scholars have taken three approaches to reconciling the conflicting passage: harmony - the passages can be harmonized; reactionary - a later writer changed the newer text in Chronicles and altered it; contradictory - the biblical accounts simply say two opposing things and are contradictory. Options two and three are somewhat ridiculous. These passages can be harmonized by the revelation from other texts concerning the relationship between the Lord and Satan and the Lord's servants.

The Book of Job unveils realities inside the relationship of Satan, the Lord, and the Lord's servants. The Lord and Satan communicate with each other about the creation of the Lord. Satan walks the earth and seeks to defile and destroy all that brings pleasure to the Lord. The Lord moved Satan to attack Job by bragging on Job, by taking pleasure in Job and by celebrating the authenticity of Job. Satan was outraged and asked for permission to prove the Lord wrong about Job. The Lord permitted Job to be attacked. Satan killed his children, destroyed his possessions, ravaged his body and disturbed the unity in his marriage. Job did not relent. Satan proceeded to turn Job's friends against him to publicly shame and dismantle his name to provoke Job to give up his integrity. Job did not give in or give up. Job endured and was restored. The Lord was glorified, and Job was proven as true and authentic. Satan was moved to attack Job because of the Lord's delight in Job, and the Lord allowed the attack in the end to do him good.

Peter's experience in Luke 22:31-32 also compliments the harmonized view. Satan asked for Peter that he might sift him and test him. The Lord permitted it. Peter failed the test, but the Lord restored him and strengthened him so that he could fall forward. Peter's denial, though famous, would propel him into the primary leadership role of the early church, which would become the greatest and largest organism in the history of human civilization. Satan was moved to attack Peter because of the Lord's delight in Peter, and the Lord allowed the attack in the end to do him good.

Paul's experience in 2 Corinthians 12 also informs us about this relationship. Paul was taken into the third heaven and saw unspeakable things related to the glory of God and wonders of our future home. A thorn in the flesh, a messenger of Satan, was given to him to hinder him. This thorn would prevent Paul from elevating and exalting himself. The thorn had a ministry and a purpose. The Lord allowed it, but it was Satan's idea. Satan attacked Paul, but the Lord permitted it. The thorn became one of Paul's greatest blessings. The grace of God proved more evident and abundant in Paul's life because of the plague of the thorn. Paul began to glory in that which he despised at first because he understood the power of God that came through his weakness. Satan was moved to attack Paul because of the Lord's delight in Paul, and the Lord allowed the attack in the end to do him good.

Who moved David? Was it the Lord? Was it Satan? You could say that they both had a role in the events. David failed the test, and the census was a sin against God. In the end, the resulting plague was stopped at Arnon the Jebusite's threshing floor. David bought that piece of property and the Temple was erected on that spot. Today this piece of ground is still the most valuable piece of property on the face of the earth, unpurchasable by wealth.

INSIGHTS FROM OTHER TEXTS

The insights gained from other texts may expose background information that enlightens the reader. In 2 Samuel 11:3, Bathsheba is introduced to the reader as the daughter of Eliam. King David sins against God and takes Bathsheba and lays with her. The introduction of Bathsheba with her father's name gives the reader access to further information about her. According to 2 Samuel 23:34, she was the granddaughter of Ahithophel, the advisor of King David. The reader can know that King David knew who she was. She was married to a non-Jewish man named Uriah the Hittite, one of David's mighty men who stood with him when nobody would. They lived in the city of David indicating that David blessed the marriage. She was the granddaughter of one of his closet counselors. After having her husband killed to cover his sin, He took Bathsheba as his wife in what would have been interpreted by the people as an extreme act of honor considering that her dead husband had no Jewish kinsman to take her and the baby she carried. Therefore, the passage in 2 Samuel 23 sheds important light on the passage in 2 Samuel 11.

Other texts may explain unknown aspects of another text. In the book of Exodus, Moses is introduced. His experience as a young man attempting to lead his people was recorded in Exodus 2:11-15. He is asked by a Hebrew in Exodus 2:14: "Who made you a prince and a judge over us?" Little is reported in Exodus about Moses' state of mind, sense of calling, and contemplations at this younger age. In Acts 7:23-25, however, the Bible exposed Moses' state of mind and motivations, "Now when he was forty years old, it came into his heart to visit his brethren, the children of Israel. And seeing one of them suffer wrong, he defended and avenged him who was oppressed, and struck down the Egyptian. For he supposed that his brethren would have understood that God would deliver them by his hand, but they did not understand." Moses walked out of the palace to begin to lead his people supposing that they would know what God had placed into his heart to do. After being rejected, Moses would spend the next forty years in the desert as an exile.

The account of Sarah in Genesis 18:12-15 records Sarah laughing at the words of the Lord when He reveals to her that she would have a child the following year at age ninety. The Lord asked Abraham why she laughed. The text seems to indicate a faithless response of Sarah upon the assurance from the Lord that she would have a child the following year. She laughed. Ironically, the child would be named Isaac, which means laughter. Sarah's faith seemed to struggle and waiver at this point. The text reveals that the way of a women had ceased to be with her. If the Genesis account was all that the reader relied upon, then it could be easily misunderstood. The writer of Hebrews clarifies this experience in Hebrews 11:11, "By faith Sarah herself received power to conceive, even when she was past the age, since she considered him faithful who had promised." Sarah's faith appeared to struggle and stumble in Genesis, but in Hebrews her faith was declared strong. A struggling faith can be a strong faith when our faith is placed in Jesus.

PROGRESSIVE REVELATION

The Bible was written over a 1500-year period. God revealed Himself progressively. The Old Testament material has prophecies and pictures of coming events and the coming Lord. The ceremonial law embedded pictures of the coming sacrifice of Jesus Christ into the sacred activities of the priesthood and the Tabernacle. These pictures of the coming event continued until the time of Christ. Paul called these Old Testament observances: Passover, the Sabbath, the Day of Atonement, the feasts and festival, the pilgrimage, and the varying offerings prescribed in Leviticus, "shadows of things to come" (Colossians 2:17). Paul stated that these were shadows of the substance which is Christ. Jesus, His sacrifice and glorious resurrection and reign was symbolized throughout the Old Testament and fully reveled in the New Testament. Paul clarified this process, "the mystery which has been hidden from ages and from generations, but now has been revealed to His saints. To them God willed to make known what are the riches of the glory of this mystery among the Gentiles: which is Christ in you, the hope of glory." As the reader studies the Old Testament, Jesus should be brought out of the shadows into the foreground. Jesus was the Passover lamb slain as our perfect sacrifice to deliver us from the plague of death. Jesus was our sinless sacrifice to bring atonement of sin.

The New Testament completed the revelation of God. Jude stated it like this, "the faith once for all delivered to the saints" (Jude 3). Paul explained that the Scripture will thoroughly furnish us for every good work (2 Timothy 3:16-17). Peter commanded that we focus on the Old Testament and the New Testament, the writings of the apostles as they gave us the commandments of the Lord Jesus (2 Peter 3:2). Other faiths, like Islam and The Church of Jesus Christ of Latter-Day Saints, claim that further revelation was needed to complete God's revelation. Muslims look to Mohammed and the Qur'an. Mormons look to the Book of Mormon and Joseph Smith. Some believe that church history provides infallible revelation to change that which was recorded in the Bible. God's revelation progressed through history until our Lord came, and He fully disclosed it to us through His apostles and their writings. Christians have but one book, the Bible. The Bible is complete and once for all the full and final revelation until He comes again. Even so, come Lord Jesus.

Chapter 8
APPLICATION

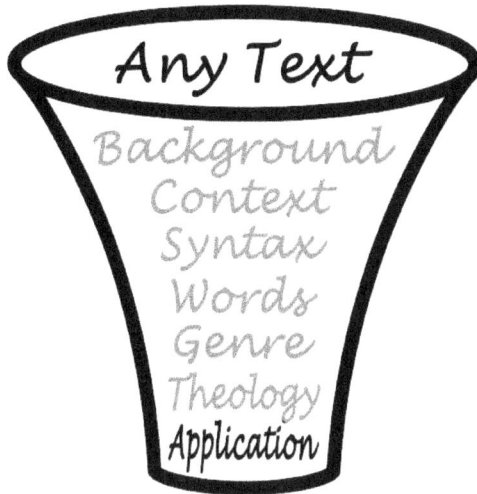

Any Text

Background
Context
Syntax
Words
Genre
Theology
Application

The final step in the funnel process involves analyzing the text for application. The previous steps have enabled the reader to understand what was said when it was written. The step of application exposes the "so what" of the text. What does this text mean to the reader today? How should it be applied? Paul explained to Timothy, "All Scripture is given by inspiration of God, and is profitable for doctrine, for reproof, for correction, for instruction in righteousness, that the man of God may be complete, thoroughly equipped for every good work." All the Bible is helpful and profitable. God moved upon men to write the Bible, inspired by the Holy Spirit, as a revelation of Himself so that we could apply it to our lives. Other religious books are believed to be transcendent and impossible to understand, interpret, and apply. The Bible exists because God wanted people to know Him, to worship Him in spirit and in truth, and to be set free through the truth. Bible study truly begins when the application starts. The Holy Spirit inspired the Bible to make lives whole, reconstruct worldviews, correct behavior, and produce growth.

The reader must be able to discover the meaning of the text and make precise application. Peter clarified for the reader that each text has an intended interpretation which is not derived by the reader, "knowing this first, that no prophecy of Scripture is of any private interpretation, for prophecy never came by the will of man, but holy men of God spoke as they were moved by the Holy Spirit" (2 Peter 1:20-21). The passage cannot be interpreted in different ways with all the interpretations being correct. God intended for the text to have one meaning. The application may vary according to the context, but the meaning is the same. Each text has one interpretation and many applications or implications.

Robert Stein discussed this in his book, *A Basic Guide to Interpreting the Bible*, and concluded that the reader does not determine the meaning of a text. He clarified and corrected the view that the reader grants the meaning to the text: "This view assumes that there are many legitimate meanings of a text, for each interpreter contributes his or her meaning to the text. The text functions somewhat like an inkblot into which the reader pours his or her own meaning."[20]

---

[20] Robert Stein, *A Basic Guide to Interpreting the Bible* (Grand Rapids: Baker, 1994), 20.

APPLICATION QUESTIONS

The reader may use a simple question guide to approach the text for application. These five questions were prescribed to be used in the beginning of the study:

1) Is there a promise to claim?

2) Is there a sin to avoid?

3) Is there a command to obey?

4) Is there a lesson to learn?

5) Is there a new truth to carry with me?

This writer first heard these questions from Dr. Adrian Rogers, who credited The Navigators for these questions.

The reader must seek to understand the original situation in the text, make a comparison to the current situation, and derive specific applications in light of the revealed will of God. Promises granted to the audience in the Bible apply to the believers in this generation. Paul stated an incredible promise in Philippians 1:6, "He who has begun a good work in you will complete it until the day of Jesus Christ." Today's church and Christian can claim this promise as their own. God started the work and will not cease until it is finished on the day of Christ. Sins are described and prohibited in the Bible, and these apply to the reader of today. Paul wrote in Ephesians 5:3, "But fornication and all uncleanness or covetousness, let it not even be named among you, as is fitting for saints." Fornication, uncleanness, or covetousness are sins to be avoided. Sex of any kind outside of the marriage covenant between a man and woman defined fornication. Fornication may be accepted in modern communities and churches, but the Bible calls it sin.

The Bible corrects, reproves, instructs, and teaches. God gave His word to apply to minds. The thinking of the church should be derived from the Bible. Doctrine is the systematic teaching of the Scripture which informs the Christian to understand how to view anything in life. In the Garden of Eden, Adam and Eve were placed there without sin. God created Adam from the dirt of the ground and returned him to work the ground. He was alone, and God said that it was not good. God fashioned Eve from Adam, placed them in the garden to be fruitful and multiply and to steward the garden. God was developing them while they were sinless. He placed a tree, the tree of the knowledge of good and evil, amidst the garden. He did not place it on a mountain or in the middle of an ocean. God placed the tree in a location that would be passed by every day. God prohibited Adam and Eve from eating from the tree, "but of the tree of the knowledge of good and evil you shall not eat, for in the day that you eat if it you shall surely die" (Genesis 2:17).

Adam and Eve looked at the tree, and the serpent, Satan, sought to shape the way in which they viewed the tree. Satan was able to convince them to desire the fruit of the forbidden tree, and they ate. The Bible instructs the reader on the way in which to view any and everything in life. Otherwise, Satan, the world, and the flesh will control perceptions and desires which lead people away from God. The Bible generates a worldview for the reader to follow.

The Bible confronts people concerning their sin. The Bible follows and reveals the divine ethic concerning all things. God's nature is pure and, therefore all His word is pure. He issues commands to obey and sins to avoid. The Ten Commandments present to the reader ten values of virtue to follow and corrupt, wicked actions to avoid. Therefore, for each sin to avoid there is a command to obey. "Thou shalt have no other Gods before me" is a sin to avoid. Love the one true God exclusively is the command to obey. "Thou shall not covet" is the sin to avoid while the command to obey is to be content with what you possess. "Thou shall not lie" is the sin to avoid while the command to obey is to tell the truth.

Many narrative texts prove to be examples of lessons in life to learn. Jesus used miracles to teach lessons. He fed the five thousand to display visually to the disciples His ability to take such meager resources and multiple them to feed the masses. The Lord is the supernatural resource. Jesus raised the dead to demonstrate His power over death and the grave as a comfort to all.

THE FIELDS OF APPLICATION

The sharp precision of Bible application cuts into the life of the individual. The Bible tells the individual the wickedness of sin and the way of salvation. The individual is enlightened from the Bible to obtain a moral framework to interpret life, liberty and the pursuit of happiness. God inspired the Scripture to help the individual build a life upon the rock of Jesus Christ in such a way that it will stand through the harsh tests of time. God blessed individuals by revealing Himself in His word. The Bible instructs the individual on financial stewardship, marital fellowship, and contextual worship. Jesus spoke to anyone who would hear his sayings and do them. He spoke to the individual. The inner circle of application must be the individual.

The individual is not the only field of application. God spoke to collectives in His word and proper application can address many collectives. God's word applies to the family. The family in America needs to hear the word of God. God provides roles to be taken in the family. The husband and father has a distinct role from the wife and mother and the children. A reader seeking to make proper application must think of the fields of application beyond the individual.

God has a revelation for the church. Many of the books of the Bible were written to churches. The book of Revelation contains seven letters to seven different churches. God speaks directly to churches in 1 Corinthians to unify and purify the body of Christ. God judges churches as a group and the individuals in those churches are weighed in the balance to inspect the works performed and the attitudes possessed. Churches are as unique as individuals. It is the church that will endure forever as our group. The family relationships of husband and wife will not persist in heaven but brothers and sisters in Christ will be in covenant with one another for all of eternity. Many commands must be obeyed in relationship to the church as we express our gifts, serve the body of Christ, partake of the Lord's Supper, report to the congregation, submit to divine authority established in the church, and missionally interact with the world. Likewise, sins of neglecting the church and collective worship involve church participation.

The Holy Spirit inspired prophets to speak to cities. Cities are collectives of people that God judges, speaks to, and seeks to reconcile to Himself. Sodom and Gomorrah, Tyre and Sidon, Ninevah, and Jerusalem are given direct and special revelation from God, messages to correct and instruct them. The reader should take note of a city or community application to love your neighbor, pray for the peace of your city, and glory in the God of the city.

Finally, the field of application extends to the government. God judges nations and governments. The people in those governments have a solemn responsibility as ministers of God according to the Apostle Paul in Romans 13. Governments exist as collective wholes responsible to God. Elijah spoke to the government and the king. John the Baptist challenged Herod's moral failure concerning his marriage to his brother's wife. Isaiah, Micah, and Amos preached and wrote to the nations around them. God is the God of all governments. He is the King of Kings and the Lord of Lords.

The reader can ask these simple questions of the different collectives to whom God speaks. Are there commands to obey for the government, for the family, for the church, or for the city? God also has promises to claim for these groups. God promised to meet the needs of churches in Philippians 4:19. God promised to bring healing to our nation in 2 Chronicles 7:14.

Chapter 9
DISCOVERING THE BIBLE

The Bible contains the richest reservoir of life-giving truth in the world. People are dying from a lack of truth. The truth contained in the Bible has the power to free people. The readers must seek the revelation that the heart so deeply hungers for in the Scripture. This book provides helpful, simple processes to read and understand the Bible. All the reader lacks is time in the Bible.

The funnel process provides a needed framework for any reader to begin to feed on the treasures found in the Bible. As the reader discovers the Bible, life change will ensue. The reader should not be surprised to find appetites change, behaviors adjust, attitudes transform, and relationships become more meaningful. As you seek the life found in the Bible, the life of Jesus will begin to flow through you.

The Bible has a main purpose: to reveal Jesus Christ to the reader. Jesus said to study the Scriptures for they testify of Me. You may not know Jesus Christ. You may have heard of Him, respect Him, and even love Him. But do you know Him? He died to save you. He came so that you may have life and have it more abundantly than you could imagine. Would you trust Him today? Would you call upon the name of Jesus today and receive Him by trusting that He died for your sin and has been raised from the dead so that you may live?

Now, take the Bible and this book as a guide to discovering it and feasting on the riches contained therein. The reader needs to share the blessings and truths that have been learned with family and friends. People die for lack of knowledge of the Bible. The reader needs to get involved in a local church to be taught the Bible and to obey the Bible.

BIBLIOGRAPHY

Beeby, W.T. *Anabaptists of the 16th Century and the Baptist of the 19th Century*. American Baptist Historical Society, 1838.

Bright, Steve. "Sabbath Keeping and the New Covenant." Christian Research Journal 26, no. 2 (2009; updated September 13, 2023). https://www.equip.org/articles/sabbath-keeping-and-the-new-covenant/.

Butler, Trent C., Marsha A. Ellis Smith, Forrest W. Jackson, Phil Logan, and Chris Church, eds. *The Holman Bible Dictionary*. Nashville: Holman, 1991.

Carson, D. A. *Exegetical Fallacies*. Grand Rapids: Baker, 2013.

Cate, Robert. *How to Interpret the Bible*. Nashville: Broadman, 1983.

Duvall J. Scott, and J. Daniel Hays. *Grasping God's Word: A Hands-on Approach to Reading, Interpreting, and Applying the Bible*. 3rd ed. Grand Rapids: Zondervan, 2020

Hanegraaff, Hank. "Sunday Sabbath: Does Sunday Observance Violate the Sabbath?" Perspectives. Christian Research Institute. March 17, 2009. https://www.equip.org/perspectives/sunday-sabbath-does-sunday-observance-violate-the-sabbath.

Mahadevan, Anand. 2022. "What a Jar of Pickles Teaches Us About Baptism." *The Gospel Coalition*. September 16, 2022. https://in.thegospelcoalition.org/blogs/enjoy-the-gospel/baptism/.

McKnight, Scot, ed. *Introducing New Testament Interpretation*. Grand Rapids: Baker, 1990.

Osborne, Grant R. *The Hermeneutical Spiral: A Comprehensive Introduction to Biblical Interpretation*. Rev. ed. Downers Grove, IL: IVP Academic, 2010.

Sakenfeld, K. D., S. E. Balentine, K. J. Kuan, E. Schuller, B. K. Blount, J. B. Green, and P.

Perkins, eds. *The New Interpreters Dictionary of the Bible D-H*. Nashville: Abingdon, 2007.

Stein, Robert H. *A Basic Guide to Interpreting the Bible: Playing by the Rules*. Grand Rapids: Baker, 2000.

Robertson, A. T. *Word Pictures in the New Testament*. Nashville: Broadman, 1930.

Stott, John R. W. *God's New Society: The Message of Ephesians*. Downers Grove, IL: InterVarsity, 1979.

Strong, James, Warren Patrick Baker, and Spiros Zodhiates. *AMG's Annotated Strong's Dictionaries*. Chattanooga, TN: AMG Publishers, 2009.

Tenney, Merrill C., ed. *The Zondervan Encyclopedia of the Bible*. Grand Rapids: Zondervan, 1976.

Thayer, Joseph H. *Thayer's Greek-English Lexicon of the New Testament*. Peabody, MA: Hendrickson, 1996.

Virkler, Henry A. *Hermeneutics: Principles and Processes of Biblical Interpretation*. Grand Rapids: Baker, 1981.

www.ingramcontent.com/pod-product-compliance
Lightning Source LLC
Chambersburg PA
CBHW060333050426
42449CB00011B/2741